Cognitive Processing Therapy for Rape Victims

Interpersonal Violence: The Practice Series

Jon R. Conte, Series Editor

In this series...

Cognitive
Processing
Therapy
for Rape
Victims

A Treatment Manual

Patricia A. Resick
Monica K. Schnicke

Interpersonal Violence:
The Practice Series

SAGE Publications
International Educational and Professional Publisher
Newbury Park   London   New Delhi

For information address:

SAGE Publications, Inc.
2455 Teller Road
Newbury Park, California 91320
E-mail: order@sagepub.com

SAGE Publications Ltd.
6 Bonhill Street
London EC2A 4PU
United Kingdom

SAGE Publications India Pvt. Ltd.
M-32 Market
Greater Kailash I
New Delhi 110 048 India

Printed in the United States of America

Library of Congress Cataloging-in-Publication Data

Resick, Patricia A.
    Cognitive processing therapy for rape victims: a treatment manual
/Patricia A. Resick, Monica K. Schnicke.
        p.   cm. —(IVPS; vol. 4)
    Includes bibliographical references.
    ISBN 0-8039-4901-4 —ISBN 0-8039-4902-2 (pbk.)
    1. Rape trauma syndrome—Treatment. 2. Cognitive therapy.
1. Schnicke, Monica K. II. Title. III. Series: Interpersonal
violence practice series; 4.
RC560.R36R47   1993
616.85'21—dc20   93-14803
                                                                    CIP

00   01   02   10   9   8   7   6   5

This book is printed on acid-free paper.

Sage Production Editor: Gillian Dickens

Contents

Part II Cognitive Processing Therapy: Session by Session

Part III Special Considerations

Acknowledgments

Cognitive Processing Therapy has evolved through an ongoing treatment research program that has been conducted by my students and myself over the past 10 years. I would like to thank, first and foremost, the courageous women who were willing to participate in our project and who have taught us about the impact of rape and about important issues in recovery. The research on which this book is based was funded by a series of grants from the University of Missouri-St. Louis. I thank the university's funding committees as well as Chair of Psychology Gary Burger and Dean E. Terrence Jones for their ongoing support. The Center for Metropolitan Studies has contributed through the release time that has been granted me as a fellow to further my research.

I would also like to acknowledge the contributions and observations of the clinical graduate students who have worked on the project or through our clinic trauma team. Monica Schnicke, my co-author, has moved from student to true colleague and contributed important components of this book with her insight and experience.

Linda Housman has served as a cotherapist for several groups, and her observations were invaluable in writing this book. She has co-authored Chapter 17. Also notable are Sherry Falsetti, Carolyn West, and Julie Morten who have served as cotherapists for our groups. In addition, I would like to thank the many undergraduate psychology students who have helped score and code data over the years. Thanks are extended to Barbara Markway for her thoughtful comments on an earlier draft of the manuscript. Great thanks are given to Jeri Albl and Michael Griffin for all their effort in producing the final document. In addition, we would both like to thank Constance Dancu and Derek Jehu for their assistance in the development of this manuscript.

I would like to acknowledge and thank my colleagues who have collaborated, inspired, supported, and provided feedback in my endeavors over the years. Particular thanks are extended to Lois Veronen, a dear friend as well as colleague, Dean Kilpatrick and his wonderful crew at the Medical University of South Carolina in Charleston, Karen Calhoun and her colleagues at the University of Georgia, and Edna Foa and her colleagues at the Medical College of Pennsylvania.

Finally, but certainly not last, I wish to thank Keith Shaw for his love and support, Marty and Matthew Shaw for their cheerful tolerance in the face of Mom's career, and my parents, Matthew and Lovina Resick, for being there for me all along.

P. A. R.

This book is the product of input from many important people, each of whom contributed in a unique and significant way. First, I wish to thank my coauthor, Patricia Resick, who has grown to become my mentor over the years, for asking me to assist her in writing this book. Her faith in my abilities and interest in my observations have made a significant impact on my clinical, academic, and emotional growth, not only as a graduate student, but also as a person.

I also want to thank all of the brave women who took risks in trusting us with their innermost feelings and reactions to a very traumatic event in their lives. They have shown us just how strong women can be both in the face and aftermath of adversity. It is their strength that continues to inspire us to search for more effective ways of helping them reach their potential following rape.

Special thanks go to Michael Trusty for offering continuous love and emotional support over the past couple of years. His unwavering confidence in me has inspired me to accomplish more than I had ever dreamed. I also want to thank Linda Housman, my best friend and colleague, for being there when I needed her. She has also played a significant role in making the CPT groups we've led together wonderfully rewarding experiences.

And, finally, I wish to thank the rest of the Schnicke family, and especially my parents, William and Naima, for offering the emotional and financial support that I needed to pursue my career goals.

M. K. S.

PART I

RAPE AND ITS AFTERMATH

1

Introduction

Rape is a crime against sleep and memory; its afterimage imprints itself like an irreversible negative from the camera obscura of dreams. . . . Violence sends deep roots into the heart; it has no seasons; it is always ripe, evergreen.

Pat Conroy, *The Prince of Tides*

Sexual assault is very prevalent in our society. Unfortunately, it has been only recently that we have realized just how common it is. Rape and attempted rape are so underreported to police that statistics based on reporting rates are virtually the tip of the iceberg. In population survey research using a variety of methods, reporting rates have varied from 5% to 9.5% (Kilpatrick, Saunders, Veronen, Best, & Von, 1987; Koss, Gidycz, & Wisniewski, 1987; Russell, 1984). Koss (1985) found that many women have experiences that meet the legal definition of rape and yet they do not define themselves as rape victims, typically because of their prior acquaintance with the assailant. In Koss's 1985 study of women who acknowledged their experiences as rape, 8% reported the crime to the police and 13% went to a rape crisis center or hospital emergency room. None of the unacknowledged rape victims reported their victimization to police, hospitals, or rape crisis centers.

Since the mid-1980s, there have been several studies conducted that have assessed the prevalence of rape using sensitive and well-developed survey methods. Russell (1984) conducted in-person interviews with a randomly selected sample of adult women in San Francisco in 1978. Of 930 women interviewed, 24% reported at least one completed rape and 31% reported at least one attempted rape. When the two types of sexual assault were combined, 44% of the sample reported having at least one attempted or completed rape. Koss, Gidycz, and Wisniewski (1987) used self-report questionnaires on a national sample of 3,187 women enrolled in universities and colleges. They found that, even with this relatively young sample, 15.4% had experiences that met the legal definition of rape and another 12.1% had experienced attempted rape.

Kilpatrick and his colleagues used a different methodology, conducting random-digit-dialing probability phone sample surveys and follow-up interviews (Kilpatrick, Saunders, Veronen, Best, & Von, 1987; Resick, Kilpatrick, Saunders, & Best, 1991). They found that 15-18% of the women experienced completed rape and 12-13% experienced attempted rape. Of the national sample of 4,009 women, 39% reported being the victim of some type of crime, and 70% of the sample reported some type of traumatic experience, including crime, disaster, or accident.

❏ Symptoms and Recovery Patterns

Sexual assault is a major, life-threatening, traumatic event from which many victims never fully recover. Many victims develop problems with depression, poor self-esteem, interpersonal difficulties, and sexual dysfunctions (see Resick, 1990, for a review). However, the most frequently observed disorder that develops as a result of sexual assault is post-traumatic stress disorder (PTSD).

In the *Diagnostic and Statistical Manual of Mental Disorders* (3rd ed., revised) (DSM-III-R) (American Psychiatric Association, 1987), there are three criteria for the diagnosis of PTSD beyond Criterion A, the stressor criterion. Criterion B describes reexperiencing phenomena: the flashbacks, nightmares, and intrusive recollections that emerge with reminders of the assault, but which also appear to emerge even when no stimuli are apparent. Criterion C consists of avoidance behaviors: avoidance of memories of the event, numbing affect, and withdrawal from activities (the latter being an overlapping symptom with depression). Criterion D represents physiological over-reactivity such as problems falling asleep, hypervigilance, exaggerated startle responses, and strong physiological reactions in the presence of reminder stimuli. The avoidance and arousal symptoms are also observed in other anxiety disorders.

One of the old DSM-III (American Psychiatric Association, 1980) criterion items for PTSD was survivor guilt. Although many Vietnam veterans experience guilt over surviving when some of their friends were killed, this criterion, as such, is not relevant to most rape victims. However, most rape victims experience guilt over what they had to do to survive, or they feel guilt and shame over having been victimized. As a means of gaining control over the experience and feeling safe about the future, rape victims look to themselves for responsibility when questioning why the event occurred: "I won't go to parties, shopping, out on dates, and so on anymore. Therefore, I will be protected from further attack."

In the first week following the assault, 94% of rape victims have been found to meet symptomatic criteria for post-traumatic stress disorder. Three months after the crime, 47% of victims still met enough criteria for a full diagnosis of PTSD (Rothbaum, Foa, Riggs, Murdock, & Walsh, 1992). Most studies have found that the greatest amount of recovery occurs within the first 3 months postcrime. After that, there is very little additional recovery (Atkeson, Calhoun, Resick, & Ellis, 1982; Calhoun, Atkeson, & Resick, 1982; Kilpatrick, Resick, & Veronen, 1981). However, in their recent study, using weekly assessments, Rothbaum et al. (1992) found that those women who developed PTSD showed no further recovery after 1 month postcrime, while those who recovered continued to show steady improvement over the 3 months of assessment. In examining the rates of PTSD following trauma in the general female population, Resnick et al. (1991) surveyed 4,009 adult women by telephone. They found

35% of rape victims reported meeting criteria for PTSD at some point in time and 9.6% still met criteria at the time of the interview.

The other major disorder that frequently co-occurs with PTSD in rape victims is depression. Although depression is also very common following rape, it does not appear to be as prevalent as PTSD. In the research on which this book is based, treatment-seeking rape victims came to therapy an average of 7 years after being raped. They were interviewed with the Structured Clinical Interview for DSM-III-R (Spitzer, Williams, & Gibbon, 1987). Of 44 rape victims who have participated in the treatment project, 95% (42) met full criteria for PTSD and 59% (26) met full criteria for major depressive disorder.

Major depressive disorder is diagnosed according to the DSM-III-R as being present if the person has five of the following symptoms (one of which must be one of the first two) for at least 2 weeks, nearly every day: (1) depressed mood most of the day, (2) loss of interest or pleasure in all or almost all activities, (3) significant weight loss or weight gain when not dieting or binge eating, (4) insomnia or hypersomnia, (5) psychomotor retardation, (6) fatigue or loss of energy, (7) feelings of worthlessness or excessive or inappropriate guilt, (8) diminished ability to think or concentrate, or (9) suicidal ideation or a suicide attempt.

There have been several research projects that have focused on the extent of depression in rape victims. Some studies have found that depressive reactions are fairly short-lived. Frank, Turner, and Duffy (1979) found that 44% of their sample of rape victims scored in the moderately or severely depressed range within the first month. In a second study, Frank and Stewart (1984) found 56% fell in the moderately or severely depressed range on the Beck Depression Inventory (BDI). With the use of a semistructured interview, 43% were diagnosed as suffering from major depressive disorder. These depressive reactions had diminished by three months postrape. Atkeson et al. (1982) found similar results. They assessed rape victims and a matched comparison sample for 1 year and found that the two groups differed at 2 weeks, 1 month, and 2 months postcrime but not thereafter. On the BDI, 75% of the victim sample reported mild to severe depressive symptoms at two weeks postcrime.

Other researchers have found more chronic depressive reactions. Kilpatrick and Veronen (1984) found differences between rape victims and nonvictims 1 year after the crime. Resick (1988) also found that rape victims reported significantly more depression than robbery victims for 18 months after victimization. In a clinical follow-up to a random population survey, Kilpatrick, Veronen, Saunders, Best, Amick-McMullan, and Paduhovich (1987) found that rape victims were more likely to be depressed than nonvictims (mean length of time postrape was 21.9 years). They also found that 8.6% of victims of one rape and 20% of victims of two rapes met criteria for major depressive disorder at the time of the interview. Forty-six percent of single incident and 80% of multiple incident victims met criteria for a lifetime diagnosis of depression.

Suicidal ideation and attempts are of serious concern when working with rape survivors, particularly in victims who have not recovered rapidly. Frank et al. (1979), found that 2.9% reported suicidal behavior in the first month following a rape, while in the Frank and Stewart study, 27% reported such behavior. However, Ellis, Atkeson, and Calhoun (1981) found that 50% of rape victims who were assessed from 1 to 16 years postrape had considered suicide. Resick, Jordan, Girelli, Hutter, and Marhoefer-Dvorak (1988) found 43% of treatment-seeking rape victims had considered suicide, while 17% had made an attempt. Kilpatrick, Best, Veronen, Amick, Villeponteaux, and Ruff (1985) reported very similar findings in a random population survey of 2,004 women. Of their sample, 19% of those who had been raped had made a suicide attempt, and 44% reported suicidal ideation.

Thus far, research has examined self-esteem problems, fear, interpersonal difficulties, and sexual dysfunctions as additional problems resulting from rape (Becker, Abel, & Skinner, 1979; Kilpatrick et al., 1981; Murphy, Amick-McMullan, Kilpatrick, Haskett, Veronen, Best, & Saunders, 1988). It may be the case, however, that these problems sometimes stem from PTSD and depression. For example, self-esteem problems are typical in depression. Also, sexual difficulties may arise because the woman who has been raped has flashbacks and intrusive recollections that are triggered by sexual contact or she avoids sexual contact to avoid such memories and related emotions. Cognitive processing therapy (CPT) focuses specifically on PTSD and depression, but it may also be an appropriate and effective intervention for these additional problems, at least for some victims.

2

Information Processing Theory and Relevant Treatments

Having been raped means to me that something I can never get back was taken from me by someone who probably doesn't even remember or care.

The person I was before no longer exists. It means that I no longer feel safe, even during daylight hours. I used to believe that rape happened to beautiful women, sometime during the night and somewhere secluded, a world away from anyone. I thought it was something that I would have to worry about only when I was an adult. My experience shattered every one of those beliefs, and now it's hard to determine what to believe—what is true and can be trusted, and what beliefs could be challenged at any moment.

Being raped means that I now will not allow myself to be relaxed enough to let loose, to let go. I have to be in control at all times and will make every effort to separate myself from a situation where I don't feel that I have some control, some way of calling the shots. I am a control freak in my relationships. This makes intimacy difficult. Separating myself reinforces the fact that I am somehow different from those around me. Physical intimacy is an absolute impossibility. The moment I am approached in a remotely intimate way, I panic, become defensive, and become enraged. Any advance is considered hostile because I feel that he is being selfish and only wants to please himself—I'm only a means to an end. I can't stand remembering what happened every time, so I draw the line and won't cross it.

Since I was raped, I do not trust men, any of them! For a while I was even afraid of my own father, a man who would never hurt anyone, let alone his own daughter. I constantly wonder if I am trusting the right people. I never saw who raped me—how can I know who looks trustworthy?

❏ Information Processing Theory

Information processing theory has been proposed recently to explain the development and maintenance of PTSD in crime victims (Chemtob, Roitblat, Hamada, Carlson, & Twentyman, 1988; Foa, Steketee, & Rothbaum, 1989; Horowitz, 1976; Jones & Barlow, 1990; McCann & Pearlman, 1990a; McCann, Sakheim, & Abrahamson, 1988).

Information processing theory had already been proposed as an explanation of depression (Beck, Rush, Shaw, & Emery, 1979; Hollon & Garber, 1988) and fear (Beck & Emery, 1985; Lang, 1977), although not within the context of criminal victimization. For a review of the literature that supports an information processing explanation of PTSD, see articles by Resick and Schnicke (1990, 1992).

Information processing theory speaks to the way in which information is encoded and recalled in memory. Humans process a vast amount of information every day. This information has to be organized and stored such that people can act on incoming information without becoming overwhelmed. One way of organizing and processing this information is through the development of schemata. A *schema* is a generic stored body of knowledge that interacts with the incoming information such that it influences how the information is encoded, comprehended, and retrieved. Schemata guide attention, expectations, interpretations, and memory searches (Williams, Watts, MacLeod, & Mathews, 1988).

If someone had a generic schema regarding rape, this schema would guide the attention to and interpretation of new information. If a woman had not experienced a rape, then her schema would most likely be formed by stereotypes and information presented in the media. Because the cases that receive attention in the news are likely to be stranger rapes, this type of information would be schema-congruent. Rapes would be likely to be viewed as assaults on other women by strangers in isolated places.

Information that did not fit this schema would most likely have been disregarded. However, when attacked herself, the woman cannot ignore this major traumatic event, but is likely to process it in light of her existing schemata. In whatever ways this event differs from her expectations and understanding of herself and the world, the woman will find herself in conflict, with no simple way to comprehend, encode, or store this most significant life event. If the assailant is an acquaintance whom she trusted, the rape will be particularly difficult to label and encode as a rape. Even if a woman were assaulted by a stranger (that is, it was schema-congruent), if she had previously believed that it could not happen to her, or if the assailant behaved in some way inconsistent with her rape schema, the rape would be difficult to integrate with her existing schema. Without a way to understand and categorize the experience, the strong emotions associated with sexual assaults are also left unprocessed.

In the sample therapy homework presented at the beginning of the chapter, the woman describes very clearly what her rape schema had been: an attack of a beautiful woman by a stranger in an isolated place at night. This schema made it difficult for her to comprehend what was happening to her. She was raped 5 years earlier at the age of 14 by a stranger in a park after a picnic. The rape was her first sexual experience. The rape not only contradicted her rape schema, but also conflicted with her schemata about sex, trust, men, and her own control and safety.

It has been fairly well established in the social psychological literature that people tend to subscribe to a just-world belief, that good things happen to good people and bad things happen to bad people (Lerner & Miller, 1978). This belief probably serves a defensive function so that people feel less vulnerable to random negative events. The occurrence of a particularly negative event, such as a rape, is schema-discrepant with this just-world belief. Hollon and Garber (1988) suggest that when an individual encounters new information that is inconsistent with preexisting beliefs or schemata, one of two things usually happens: assimilation or accommodation.

Assimilation refers to the process whereby information is altered or distorted to fit (to be assimilated) into existing schemata. Accommodation, on the other hand, involves changing existing schemata to accept new, incompatible information.

In rape victims, assimilation is frequently observed when the victims blame themselves for being attacked or not resisting successfully, question whether the event was really a rape, or develop an amnesia for all or part of the event. The following statements written by rape victims in therapy illustrate assimilation.

> Sometimes I think I don't quite know what being raped means to me. After four months, I still feel confused and unsure about the whole thing. I was in such a fog after it happened that I think the reality of the situation is just beginning to hit me.

> Because I felt it was my own fault, because I used poor judgment, I no longer trust myself and my decisions. It was easier for me to blame myself than the rapist, and so I still have a hard time getting to the anger that I know is buried. Intimacy is difficult because I can't ever let anyone know the "real" me, I am busy pretending to be someone else to be accepted.

Accommodation, which is necessary for successful integration of the event, may not be successful for symptom reduction if the victim completely alters her view of the world in ways that prevent intimacy or trust and increase fear (overaccommodation). Although Hollon and Garber did not suggest overaccommodation, we have certainly observed it—almost universally—in rape victims. The first example at the beginning of the chapter illustrates overaccommodation, changes in beliefs and schemata to the extreme. After the rape, the woman never felt safe, trusted no one, and felt she had to be in control of herself and her relationships all of the time.

The therapist's job is to assist with the integration of the event, with complete processing of emotions and accommodation of schemata, while helping the client maintain or achieve a healthy outlook, a balanced perception of the world. When information is not processed adequately, intrusive recollections, flashbacks, and nightmares are likely to occur. These intrusive symptoms are associated with strong affective responses, which then lead to escape and avoidance behavior such as avoiding situations that remind her of the event.

Cognitive avoidance—refusing to accept what has occurred or to integrate the event into one's life experiences—prevents the extinction of strong affective responses (fear, guilt, disgust, and anger). Memories, which have been encoded in rich detail because they were so schema-discrepant (Hollon & Garber, 1988), continue to elicit great affect when they are activated by stimuli in the environment. Fear cues, in particular, can generalize and create symptoms of chronic arousal and hyperreactivity.

A substantial percentage of rape victims also experience significant depression in the aftermath of the event (Atkeson, Calhoun, Resick, & Ellis, 1982; Frank & Stewart, 1984; Kilpatrick, Resick, & Veronen, 1981; Resick, 1988). Again, an information processing model of depression appears to fit these data. When assimilation and accommodation occur such that the victim blames herself for the event, yet feels helpless and hopeless about recovering or preventing other traumas, depression is a likely outcome.

Preexisting beliefs and events that occurred prior to the rape may have a profound effect on how the event is processed. Early losses and traumas may result in negative schemata (for example, "Bad things keep happening to me") that appear to be confirmed by the rape. In contrast, an overly sheltered childhood may result in unrealistic just-world schemata (for example, "As long as I follow the rules, nothing bad will ever happen to me") that may be shattered in the face of personal victimization. McCann and colleagues (McCann, Sakheim, & Abrahamson, 1988; McCann & Pearlman, 1990a) have proposed that specific symptoms are developed if prior positive schemata are disrupted or negative schemata are seemingly confirmed by victimization.

With regard to content, McCann et al. have identified five major areas of functioning, or *themes*, that are affected and disrupted by victimization: *safety, trust, power, esteem,* and *intimacy.* Each area of concern is further divided into two loci: schemata related to the self and schemata related to others. For example, *self-safety* focuses on a person's beliefs that she can protect herself, and *other-safety* refers to her beliefs about the safety or dangerousness of others. While the

McCann et al. theory is new and has not yet been empirically tested, the five major areas of psychological and interpersonal functioning have face-valid heuristic value and appear to be good focal areas for therapy.

❏ **Cognitive and Behavioral Treatments for Rape Victims**

In their discussion of information processing theory in PTSD, Foa and colleagues (Foa, Steketee, & Rothbaum, 1989; Foa & Kozak, 1986) consider how established fear structures (schemata) can be dismantled. They propose that the following two conditions are necessary for the reduction of fear: (1) that the fear memory be activated, and (2) that new information be provided that is incompatible with that in the current fear structure in order for a new memory to be formed. Activation can occur through any of the three network elements: information about the stimuli, responses, or meaning. They recommend the use of some type of exposure-based therapy to achieve this goal.

When Resick, Jordan, Girelli, Hutter, and Marhoefer-Dvorak (1988) compared stress inoculation training (SIT), assertion training, and supportive therapy plus information, we found that all three types of therapy were equally effective. Stress inoculation is a treatment package that is geared toward fear-management training. It includes relaxation training, coping statements, thought-stopping, and other coping techniques. Assertion training was implemented because it had been proposed that assertive responses could be used to countercondition fear (Wolpe, 1969) and because rape victims have a great number of interpersonal concerns after the assault (for example, who to tell, how to handle people's reactions, and so on). Supportive therapy is the type of counseling most often found in rape crisis centers, and it consists of client-centered group or individual counseling. In this study, the first session of all three groups included information about rape reactions and a behavioral theory of why these symptoms develop. We proposed that the lack of differences between the three types of therapy was due to the fact that all three types of therapy provided corrective information. Although two of the groups were given skills designed to facilitate the break-up of avoidance patterns, all three groups were given a cognitive-behavioral formulation of their reactions. The explanation they received was that victims typically avoid cues (stimuli) because they trigger fear reactions but that these cues are not good indicators of actual danger. They were then given ample opportunity over the course of therapy to observe which cues triggered their reactions and to analyze the actual dangerousness of those cues (even when that was not the expressed purpose of the group). They were also given information regarding just-world theory as an explanation for why some people (including themselves) tended to blame the victim for the rape.

Frank, Anderson, Stewart, Dancu, Hughes, and West (1988) compared systematic desensitization and Beckian cognitive therapy for depression with immediate and delayed treatment seekers and found that both types of therapy were equally effective. However, there were several problems with the study. Because there was no waiting-list control group, it was not possible to determine whether the immediate treatment was more effective than the natural recovery typically reported in the first 3 months after rape. There was no assessment of PTSD symptoms. The cognitive therapy that was used had been developed for depression and focused on three target problems that the participants chose. It is quite likely that this form of cognitive therapy would not qualify as an exposure-based treatment because there was no emphasis on eliciting memories of the event or breaking up avoidance patterns. However, it is likely that the therapy did provide corrective information.

Foa, Rothbaum, Riggs, and Murdock (1991) have compared the efficacy of SIT, prolonged exposure (PE), supportive counseling (SC), and a waiting-list (WL) control group. At posttreatment, they found all four groups improved significantly (including the WL group), but SIT improved significantly more than SC and WL on PTSD symptoms. All four groups improved equally on the Rape Aftermath Symptom Test, the State-Trait Anxiety Inventory, and the Beck Depression Inventory. A second analysis comparing SIT, PE, and SC from posttherapy to 3 months follow-up indicated PE subjects continued to improve with regard to PTSD symptoms, while SIT showed no change and SC improved marginally.

In examining specific PTSD symptoms, the researchers found that SIT subjects became more symptomatic from posttreatment to follow-up on intrusive symptoms, while PE subjects continued to improve on intrusive and arousal symptoms. There was no change from posttest to follow-up on any other measure.

The authors concluded that, in the short run, SIT was more effective, while over time PE was more effective for relieving symptoms of PTSD. They hypothesized that SIT participants did not persist in employing their anxiety-management techniques after treatment ended, while PE produced more permanent changes because the PE procedures lead to enduring changes in the trauma memory (habituation to feared stimuli, reevaluation of probability of threat in feared situations, and changes in the negative valence associated with fear responses). It should be noted that neither SIT nor PE were superior to supportive counseling or waiting list on other measures of fear, anxiety, or depression.

Unfortunately, none of these studies found these therapies to be completely effective. Although statistical group comparisons are helpful, some clinical assessment is also important to determine how many subjects improve by some clinically significant amount.

Resick et al. (1988) reported that 33% of the subjects improved at least 1 standard deviation (SD) on several of the measures examined, while half of the subjects improved at least .5 SD. Frank et al. (1988) reported that approximately 63% of the delayed treatment seekers scored within 1 SD of a sample of nonvictims on measures of anxiety and depression following treatment. Foa et al. (1991) reported that all SIT subjects improved considerably and that 75% of PE subjects improved from pre- to posttreatment but did not define how much was "considerable."

❏ Overview of Cognitive Processing Therapy

Kilpatrick and Calhoun (1988) have recommended that "it might be far more productive to develop new treatments specifically tailored to the needs of victims than to continue attempting to find effects of existing treatment procedures that may be weak at best"

(p. 427). Based on the results of prior treatment studies, the recent theoretical work on information processing theory, and considerable clinical experience, we have developed a therapy designed to facilitate the integration of the traumatic event with previously constructed schemata.

The goal of the treatment is to assist the client in refraining from assimilating (distorting the event to fit prior beliefs) and in accommodating schemata to the new information without overaccommodating. For example, in the excerpt at the beginning of the chapter, it is clear that the woman is having difficulty accepting that the rape happened because it did not fit her image. However, she is also overaccommodating with safety ("It means that I am no longer safe, even during daylight hours"), trust ("Since I was raped, I do not trust men, any of them!"), power ("I have to be in control at all times"), and intimacy ("Physical intimacy is an absolute impossibility"). The therapist's goal is to have the clients remember the rape, accept that it happened, and experience their emotions about it. The clients need to attain a better balance in their beliefs about themselves and the world so everything else is not viewed with respect to the rape (for example, "No one can be trusted; I can never be safe").

Although both cognitive and exposure-based therapies have been attempted with rape victims, CPT combines both approaches with material especially tailored for rape victims. The result is a specific treatment package consisting of exposure to the traumatic memory, training in challenging cognitions, and modules on the topics that are most likely to be affected by the rape.

An approach such as CPT, which elicits memories of the event and then directly confronts conflicts and maladaptive beliefs, may be more effective than prolonged exposure alone.

Prolonged exposure activates the memory structure but does not provide direct corrective information regarding misattributions or other maladaptive beliefs. CPT, specifically designed for treatment of PTSD as well as depression in rape victims, might provide another means for activating the memory structure. Once activated, the focus of processing would include conflicting beliefs and meanings attributed to the event, as well as expectations regarding the future, that might not be elicited with other forms of exposure therapy.

While similar in many ways, cognitive processing therapy (CPT) is different than Beckian cognitive therapy (CT) in several respects. Rather than assuming that the rape elicits previously existing distorted and dysfunctional thinking patterns in the case of depression (Beck et al., 1979) or danger schemata in the case of fear and PTSD (Beck & Emery, 1985; Chemtob et al., 1988; Foa et al., 1989), we are proposing that the symptoms of PTSD are usually caused by conflict between this new information and prior schemata. These conflicts may be concerned with danger and safety ("I thought I was safe in my own bed, now I feel in danger"), but they could reflect conflicts on other themes, such as self-esteem ("There must have been something wrong with me that I was raped"), power and control ("I don't feel capable of making decisions for myself now; I'm afraid of making a mistake"), or intimacy ("I feel distant from other people now. They don't understand what I have been through"). These cognitive conflicts could account for the intrusive, arousal, and avoidance symptoms observed in PTSD. Therefore, while there are modules included to introduce the concept of faulty thinking patterns and assumptions, most of the focus of CPT is on identifying and modifying *stuck points*, or inadequately processed conflicts between prior schemata and this new information (that is, the rape).

Stuck points may arise following the appraisal of an event, based on faulty thinking patterns, or result from conflict between the rape and prior schemata, but it is also possible that: (1) negative, conflicting schemata are imposed by others (that is, blaming comments from those expected to provide support), (2) the client's coping style is avoidant and so she is unable to process the event in a complete manner (that is, she has been taught to not think about unpleasant events), or (3) there is literally no relevant schema in which to store this new information (that is, the event is so outside the range of her experience and beliefs that it cannot be comprehended). Traditional CT was not designed to deal with such circumstances.

Beck's cognitive therapy tends to deemphasize the expression of emotions. In contrast, CPT encourages clients to feel and attend to their emotions. One of the symptom clusters of PTSD is avoidance, including avoidance of strong affect. Following traumatic events, victims have overwhelming emotions that they attempt to suppress or avoid. Perceptions and beliefs about the traumatic event could be reasonably accurate but so horrifying that victims cannot reconcile the event with their prior beliefs about the world and human behavior. If successful at avoiding, many rape victims describe a complete numbing of affect. In CPT, there is an exposure component in which clients are encouraged to activate their schema of the event and to experience their emotions. They are then taught to differentiate accurate interpretations from faulty cognitions. By combining the exposure technique with deliberate focus on possible faulty or conflicting beliefs, we are attempting to locate stuck points, or areas of incomplete processing.

Another difference between CPT and CT is that Beckian therapy for depression usually begins with monitoring of daily activities and graded assignments in order to increase the client's activity level. Our experience is that these techniques are not necessary with rape victims. Even though many of the women seeking therapy are depressed as well as having PTSD, in their effort to avoid thinking about the event or as an excuse to avoid a social or sexual life, they are typically extremely busy, working overtime or on second jobs, or going to school while working.

CPT has been developed to help victims of rape (1) understand how thoughts and emotions are interconnected, (2) accept and integrate the rape as an event that actually occurred and cannot be ignored or discarded, (3) experience fully the range of emotions attached to the rape, (4) analyze and confront maladaptive beliefs, and (5) explore how prior experiences and beliefs both affected reactions and were affected by this trauma.

❑ Using This Manual

This manual gives a session-by-session outline of skills to be taught, issues to be discussed, and homework to be assigned. Successful use requires that the therapist has had training in a cognitive approach to therapy and that the therapist is familiar with typical reactions to rape. Beck and Emery (1985) and Resick (1990) are recommended background reading.

The therapy begins with a cognitive information processing explanation of rape reactions, a simplified version of information processing theory. The client is asked to begin by writing about the meaning of the event or what it means to her that she was raped. She is then taught to identify four basic feelings (mad, sad, glad, and scared) and is given illustrations of how changes in self-statements result in changes in emotions. The client is asked to analyze some events using Ellis's A-B-C sheets (adapted from Ellis and Harper, 1975). Then for several weeks, the client is asked to write about the traumatic event several times in as much detail as possible and to read the account repeatedly. (It is our experience that written accounts are far more detailed and affectively rich than oral accounts). Writing about and then reading about the rape serves as an exposure technique in that the memories and affects are activated, which should facilitate extinction of strong negative emotions.

The written accounts also give the therapist clues as to stuck points, which are conflicts produced by parts of the event that are horrifying and unacceptable to the victim. These beliefs often need the greatest active intervention by the therapist. The client may need information regarding typical victim reactions, including that others would not have been able to predict that a rape was imminent, that their reactions are normal, and that they are not going crazy. In this sense, writing also serves to facilitate accommodation of schemata.

The next series of sessions are spent developing more skills to analyze and confront maladaptive self-statements regarding the rape. The client is given a list of questions to ask herself in confronting her maladaptive beliefs (from Beck and Emery, 1985). She is introduced to Beck's concept of faulty thinking patterns and is given an exercise to complete. She is then given a new, more detailed worksheet (adapted from Beck & Emery, 1985) that she will use throughout the remainder of therapy to analyze and confront maladaptive self-statements, stuck points, and negative beliefs in the five areas of functioning.

Over the next five sessions, the client is asked to consider the five areas of psychological and interpersonal functioning that have been suggested by McCann et al. (1988), one for each session. The five topics are safety, trust, power and control, esteem, and intimacy. The client is given a handout to read on each topic, and during the following session she and the therapist discuss how these areas of functioning have been affected by the rape and how prior experiences and beliefs in these areas have played a role. The client and therapist use the handouts (list of questions, faulty thinking patterns, challenging beliefs worksheets) to examine and confront maladaptive thoughts and patterns of thinking. Homework assignments include the use of these handouts to confront stuck points on these issues and other remaining stuck points regarding the rape. In addition, one of the last homework assignments is to have the client rewrite what the meaning of the rape is now for her and to reflect on how this account differs from the one she wrote after the first session. The last session is used for review and planning for the future.

3

Diagnosis and Assessment

❏ Screening

When a woman first calls seeking treatment, she may be reluctant
to say what has happened to her on the phone. Because we special-
ize in the treatment of trauma reactions, we can ask immediately
if the caller has been victimized. This may be more difficult to
broach immediately if the therapist has a general practice. However,
a straightforward, matter-of-fact approach is recommended, particularly if the woman is having difficulty stating why she is calling
for therapy. Once she affirms that she has been victimized, the
therapist can ask when it occurred. This is important, because the
therapist will need to respond differently depending on whether the
crime was committed very recently or occurred months or years
ago, and whether the client is an incest survivor.

Regardless of the time frame since the assault, the therapist should
screen for suicidal ideation if the client is in crisis or sounds particularly depressed. As mentioned in Chapter 1, suicidal ideation is

fairly common in rape victims. It is possible that suicidal thoughts have precipitated the phone call for treatment. If this is the case, the therapist and client will need to make an oral contract until they can meet or the therapist may need to consider hospitalization if the client cannot ensure that she will be safe until the session.

If the client is an incest survivor who has been raped, we offer individual treatment and/or referrals to incest survivor groups. It has been our practice to exclude those with an incest history from rape groups, even though they may have been raped subsequently. Given that CPT is short-term treatment, it is probably not going to be beneficial for those with an incest history because of the great length of time needed for them to begin to trust the therapist and other group members and the greater likelihood of additional psychopathology (for example, personality disorders). It may also be difficult for the client to focus only on the rape without triggering unresolved incest-related issues. However, we have begun offering CPT to incest-rape survivors in an individual format with a referral for incest-related issues following CPT. The focus, however, is still on the rape. This has worked well so far. Two thirds of the subjects treated individually with CPT had histories of child sexual abuse (see Chapter 20).

If there is no reported history of incest and the crime occurred some time ago, the therapist may want to ask if something has happened recently that precipitated the client's call. If there is no crisis situation to deal with, a session can be scheduled with only brief telephone contact. Even without a discussion of symptoms, the therapist should inform the client that she may experience an increase in symptoms before the first session and that she may have the urge to avoid the session. Tell the client to come to the session regardless of how she is feeling. Inform her that avoidance makes recovery take longer. If the rape occurred many years ago, remind the client gently that what she has been doing (avoiding) has not been working, and that even though the idea of talking and thinking about the event is frightening, it will get easier. Rape victims have very high no-show rates unless this is discussed and normalized.

When someone calls within the first week after a rape, the therapist needs to respond to the crisis situation, provide immediate information, and intervene more directly on the telephone. If the victim calls very soon after the rape, it is appropriate to ask whether she has reported the crime to the police. Although reporting the crime is a woman's own personal decision, she should be aware that if the rape is not reported very soon after it was committed, she probably will not be able to press charges later. Also, in our state (Missouri), rape victims are eligible for victim compensation funds, which pay for therapy and medical expenses, but only if they report the crime within 48 hours. Therapists should be aware of laws in their own states regarding victim compensation.

Finally, the woman's decision not to report the rape to the police may indicate to the therapist that the client is struggling with issues of self-blame, is concerned that she will not be believed, or is trying to avoid labeling the event as a rape or as a crime (assimilation). This information may help the therapist to begin to formulate the client's stuck points.

Recent victims, whether they report the crime or not, should be urged to seek medical attention. Internal injuries, potential pregnancy, and venereal diseases (including AIDS) are all potential effects that need to be addressed in the aftermath of a sexual assault. Women need to be examined and treated twice—immediately after the crime and several weeks later. AIDS testing will need to be done 6 months after the crime, and the woman will need to be instructed in safe-sex practices until she knows that she has not contracted the virus.

The therapist is also in a position to help prevent the development of PTSD in that she or he can provide normalizing information about symptoms and their course, help the client activate her social support network, and help intervene with potentially damaging cognitions ("It wasn't your fault!"). Clients should be urged to feel their feelings and to talk about the crime and their reactions as much as possible. It will be possible for them to receive better social support immediately after the rape than months or years later when others will not understand why they are still upset.

❑ Initial Interview

Although we have a standardized initial interview for data collection purposes, an unstructured interview is sufficient for clinical purposes. The first purpose of the initial interview is to gather information about the incident, reactions to the assault, social support, and history of other traumatic events. A second purpose is to begin normalizing reactions. Most rape victims arrive at therapy with the secret belief that they are going crazy. Asking about PTSD symptoms and labeling them accurately (flashbacks rather than hallucinations) helps to alleviate the client's concern that she is having a uniquely bad reaction.

A calm, supportive, matter-of-fact manner on the part of the therapist also leads to rapport building and to the expectation on the part of the client that her problems are not insurmountable. This therapist reaction, the third purpose of the interview, serves as a corrective reaction to others' negative reactions. If the therapist does not react with shock, blame, fear, and so on, then she or he is sending the message that this event is not too big to handle. Unfortunately, we have seen too many clients who have come from other therapists who have reacted in a negative and damaging fashion by either overreacting to or ignoring the clients' disclosure.

❏ Assessment

We are strong believers in assessment. Aside from using assessment measures to conduct large-scale studies, we also conduct assessments with the clients we see in therapy who are not part of our research studies. Furthermore, we assess clients at the end of and sometimes during treatment, as well as at the beginning of therapy. At the beginning of therapy, it is important to determine the level of symptomatology, or the extent of distress the client is experiencing. The presence of depression as well as PTSD may indicate more pervasive patterns of cognitive disruption, more problems with self-esteem, and greater hopelessness. Of the PTSD symptoms, we hope to see greater intrusion and relatively less avoidance. This suggests that the client is actively processing the event (even though she might be stuck or distressed) and is not avoiding her affect. If the client scores high on avoidance but low on intrusion, then she may not have the event in active memory and is likely using a coping style that is more resistant to therapy. The therapist may have to work with the client more to help her overcome her long-term tendencies to avoid her affect and cognitions, not just regarding the rape, but also on other topics.

We have learned through experience that it is often helpful for the client to see objectively the progress she is making in therapy. Sometimes during therapy, a client will become so preoccupied with a particular stuck point or with more general issues (for example, esteem or intimacy) that she may not notice that she is no longer having flashbacks, intrusive recollections, or numbing of affect. By conducting a reassessment, during and at the end of therapy, both the client and the therapist can see the progress she has made. On the other hand, no change in scores may indicate to the therapist that core constructs have not changed and that the therapist may have to probe behind superficial stuck points for larger maladaptive core assumptions. Pronounced avoidance may indicate a core assumption that emotions are bad and should not be experienced or that they are so overwhelming that the client cannot cope with them.

The assessment battery we are currently using in our research project is as follows: Structured initial interview; Structured Clinical Interview for DSM-III-R—Nonpatient Version, Mood Disorders, and PTSD Modules; PTSD Symptom Scale; Impact of Event Scale; Symptom Checklist-90-Revised; Beck Depression Inventory; Hopelessness Scale; and Causal Dimension Scale.

STRUCTURED INITIAL INTERVIEW

The structured initial interview (Resick, 1988) we use contains the following sections: Demographics, Sexual Assault Information, Social Support, History of Victimization, Psychological History, and Problems and Treatment Since Crime. The purpose of the interview is to attempt to determine the factors that have affected the severity of the woman's reactions and those that have facilitated or hindered her recovery from the crime. For example, negative reactions from others may compound the trauma and increase trust and intimacy difficulties, as well as self-blame.

STRUCTURED CLINICAL INTERVIEW FOR DSM-III-R—NONPATIENT
VERSION (SCID), MOOD DISORDERS, AND PTSD MODULES

The SCID (Spitzer, Williams, & Gibbons, 1987) was developed to
assess Axis I disorders based on the DSM-III-R criteria. The depression and PTSD modules are used to make a formal diagnosis of both
lifetime and current depressive or PTSD disorders.

PTSD SYMPTOM SCALE (PSS)

The PSS (Foa, Riggs, Dancu, & Rothbaum, in press) has 17 items
and two versions: interview and self-report. The scale is based
directly on the DSM-III-R criteria for PTSD and has three subscales
that reflect the three major symptom criteria: intrusion, avoidance,
and arousal. It is a very easy scale both to administer and understand, has good concurrent validity with the SCID and IES (below),
and has good test-retest reliability.

IMPACT OF EVENT SCALE (IES)

The IES (Horowitz, Wilner, & Alvarez, 1979) is a 15-item self-
report scale that consists of two subscales measuring cognitive
intrusion and avoidance. Although the IES cannot be used to diag-
nose PTSD because it measures only cognitive intrusion and avoidance and does not assess arousal symptoms, it is a widely used scale
in the trauma literature. In addition, the subscales can give the
clinician a good idea of the relative strength of intrusive versus
avoidant symptoms.

SYMPTOM CHECKLIST-90-REVISED (SCL-90-R)

The SCL-90-R (Derogatis, 1977) is a 90-item Likert self-report scale
that measures the level of overall distress and has nine subscales
with the original scoring. These subscales assess somatization,
obsessive-compulsive symptoms, interpersonal sensitivity, depression, anxiety, hostility, phobic anxiety, paranoid ideation, and psychoticism. An additional PTSD scale was developed by Saunders,
Arata, and Kilpatrick (1990) from the original 90 items. The SCL-90-R

has been used widely in rape research and provides good norms for typical responses following rape (Kilpatrick, Resick, & Veronen, 1981; Resick et al., 1988). Clinicians using the scale should be aware that high scores on paranoia and psychoticism subscales are quite common in rape victims with PTSD and are not indicative of severe pathology. Symptoms of PTSD are likely to elevate scores on those two subscales because rape victims are suspicious and lacking in trust (someone was out to get them!), and flashbacks are often perceived and labeled as hallucinations, so strange experiences are endorsed on the psychoticism scale.

BECK DEPRESSION INVENTORY (BDI)

The BDI (Beck, Ward, Mendelson, Mock, & Erbaugh, 1961) is the most widely used self-report scale for measuring depressive symptoms. This 21-item scale has established cutoffs for measuring the severity of depression and norms for rape victims measured over time (Atkeson, Calhoun, Resick, & Ellis, 1982).

HOPELESSNESS SCALE

Although the Hopelessness Scale (Beck, Weissman, Lester, & Trexler, 1974) was developed to measure cognitive appraisals in depression, it was used in our research to assess changes in cognitions generally. There are three subscales: feelings about the future, loss of motivation, and future expectations.

CAUSAL DIMENSION SCALE

The Causal Dimension Scale (Russell, 1982) was also used to assess cognitions—but in this case, causal attributions regarding the crime. The scale was originally developed to assess three dimensions: controllable-uncontrollable, internal-external, and stable-unstable. We divided the controllability dimension into two additional loci: controllable by you and controllable by others, because at least two people are present in a rape who could have some control.

Because the typical reactions to rape are post-traumatic stress disorder (PTSD) and depression, the assessment measures we use have focused primarily on these two diagnoses. In addition, because we have been examining an information processing model of PTSD, we typically include several cognitive measures. All participants are assessed prior to starting treatment and 1 week and 3 and 6 months following treatment. Because this information was collected as part of a research project, the battery is quite extensive and typically takes 3 hours to administer.

For clinical purposes, we recommend the following battery for diagnosis and assessment of PTSD and depression:

- Initial interview
- PTSD Symptom Scale
- Beck Depression Inventory

Both of the scales take only minutes to administer and score and provide a good indication of the severity of PTSD and depressive symptomotology. Means and standard deviations on the assessment measures pre- and posttreatment are presented in Chapter 20. These means and standard deviations can be used to compare how one's individual client compares to the typical rape victim entering and completing therapy.

PART II

*COGNITIVE PROCESSING
THERAPY:
SESSION BY SESSION*

4

Session 1: Introduction and Education Phase

Overall, the goals for the first session are to educate the client regarding symptoms of post-traumatic stress disorder (PTSD) and depression and information processing theory, to lay out the course of treatment, and to elicit treatment compliance. It is necessary to address compliance because avoidance behavior (a symptom of PTSD) can interfere with successful treatment. We are concerned with two forms of compliance: attendance and completion of homework assignments. It is strongly recommended that clients attend all sessions and complete all assignments in order to benefit fully from therapy. We attempt to set the expectation that therapy benefit depends on the amount of effort they invest through homework compliance and practice with new skills.

Clients are also given the opportunity to ask any questions they may have about rape or therapy. Sometimes clients' stuck points become evident in the questions and concerns they express during the first session. And finally, as with all therapies, rapport building is crucial for effective therapy. The client needs to feel understood and listened to, otherwise she may not return.

If the therapist has not conducted an assessment session, she or he will need to find out what happened to the client and what her reactions are. Even with a prior assessment session, clients sometimes arrive with a press to speak about their story. They may have waited for a long time to share their story with someone and should be given the opportunity to do so. Other clients will be very reluctant to discuss the rape and will be quite relieved that they do not have to describe it in detail during the first session. An initial assessment session grants the client and therapist the opportunity to get acquainted before the therapy actually begins and allows the therapist to provide the client with a description of what the therapy will entail.

If no initial assessment is conducted, it is important that the therapist inform the client that this is a very structured form of therapy, and that this session is a bit different from the others because the therapist will do more talking than usual. The therapist begins with a cognitive formulation of PTSD:

In going over the results of your testing, we found that you are suffering from post-traumatic stress disorder. The symptoms of PTSD fall into three clusters. The first cluster is the reexperiencing of the event in some way. This includes nightmares about the crime or other scary dreams; flashbacks, when you act or feel as if the incident is recurring; or intrusive thoughts, which are memories that suddenly pop into your mind. You might have the intrusive thoughts when there is something in the environment to remind you of the crime (including anniversaries of the crime) or even when there is nothing there to remind you of it. Common times to have these memories are when you are falling asleep, when you relax, or when you are bored. These symptoms are all normal following such a traumatic event. You are not going crazy. Can you give me examples of these experiences in your own life since the event?

The second cluster of symptoms is avoidance of reminders of the event. You might avoid places or people who remind you of the crime. Some women avoid watching certain television programs or turn off the TV when violence is on. Some women avoid reading the newspaper or watching the news. You might avoid thinking about the event and letting yourself feel your feelings about the crime. There might be certain sights, sounds, or smells that you find yourself avoiding or escaping from because they remind you of the rape. Some women have trouble being touched or avoid dating or sex. Sometimes people have trouble remembering all or part of the crime. Sometimes women feel numb and cut off from the world around them. This feeling of detachment or numbness is another form of avoidance. Sometimes it is described as feeling as though you are watching life from behind glass. Which things or thoughts do you avoid or run away from? Have you felt numb or shut off from your emotions?

The third set of symptoms concerns arousal. These symptoms include problems falling or staying asleep, irritability or outbursts of anger, difficulty concentrating, startle reactions like jumping at noises or if someone walks up behind you, always feeling on guard or looking over your shoulder even when there is no reason to, and strong physical reactions when something in the environment reminds you of the crime. Which of these do you experience?

Now I would like to explain why you developed these symptoms. When you were growing up you learned about the world and organized it into categories or beliefs. For example, when you were small, you learned that a thing with a back, seat, and four legs is a chair. In the beginning you just called all of them "chair." Later, as you got older, through experience, you learned more complex categories, so you may have learned dining room chair, rocking chair, recliner, or folding chair. We develop many categories for ideas and beliefs as well as for objects.

One common belief that many people have is that "good things happen to good people and bad things happen to bad people." This is called the "just-world belief." You may have learned this through your religion or your parents, or you may have picked it up as a way to make the world seem safer and more predictable. If you have ever had things go bad and you said "Why me?," then you have a just-world belief. What did you believe about rape before it happened to you?

Some women report that they had never thought about it. If so, the therapist can point out that they did not have a category in their head in which to put this experience.

When an unexpected event occurs that doesn't fit your beliefs, one of two things usually happens. You either change your memories or interpretation of the event to fit your beliefs, or you change your beliefs about the world and these events. Examples of changing your interpretations or memories of the event are to blame yourself for not preventing the rape, to question whether the event was really a rape, to "forget" that it happened, or to forget the most horrifying parts. Many women can't even say that it was a rape or use that word. Changing the event is easier than changing your entire set of beliefs about the world, how people behave, or your beliefs about your safety.

It is possible that instead of changing the event, you may change your beliefs to accept what happened. This is one of our goals for therapy. Unfortunately, many women go overboard and change their beliefs too much, which may result in a reluctance to become intimate or develop trust and increased fear. Examples that reflect an extreme change in beliefs include: thinking that no man can be trusted or that the world is completely dangerous. Our goals for therapy are (1) to help you accept that the rape occurred, (2) to help you change your beliefs enough to accept it without going overboard, and (3) to feel your feelings about it.

The fourth goal of therapy will be to help you recognize and modify what you are saying to yourself—in other words, your thoughts and interpretations about the rape, which may have become automatic. Sometimes when an event occurs that doesn't fit your beliefs about the world and people, you may distort the facts to fit your beliefs. These distorted beliefs may become so automatic that you aren't even aware that you have them. Even though you may not be aware of what you are saying to yourself, your beliefs and self-statements affect your mood. Often, people aren't aware that they are having thoughts about whatever they are experiencing. For example, on the way here today, you were probably wondering what this therapy would be like or what I would be asking you to talk about. Do you remember what you were thinking about before the session?

I will be helping you to identify what your automatic thoughts are and how they influence what you feel. I will also teach you ways to challenge and change what you are saying to yourself and what you believe about yourself and the event. Some of your beliefs about the crime will be more accurate than others. We will be focusing on changing the beliefs that are interfering with your recovery. These problematic beliefs are called "stuck points."

The client is given the handout on stuck points.

I cannot emphasize enough how important it is that you not avoid, which is what you usually have done to try to cope since the rape. This will be your biggest (and probably scariest) hurdle. I cannot help you feel your feelings, or challenge your thoughts if you don't come to therapy or if you avoid completing homework assignments. If you find yourself wanting to avoid, remind yourself that you are still struggling with the rape because you have avoided dealing with it head on.

For homework until the next session, I would like you to start paying attention to what you say to yourself and to write down your thoughts about and interpretations of the rape. In other words, I want you to write about what it means to you that you were raped. How has it changed your view of yourself, other people, and the world in general? In order for this assignment to be most helpful to you, I strongly suggest you try to start this assignment soon so that you have enough time to write thoughtfully. Pick a time and place where you have as much privacy as possible so you can feel any feelings that arise as you complete the assignment.

The client is given a homework sheet. If the client feels uncomfortable writing, the therapist might suggest that she record her thoughts into a tape recorder. Chapters 2 and 5 contain examples of this assignment as completed by clients.

Examples of homework are given in the chapters in which they are discussed with the client rather than in the chapter in which the homework was assigned. The usual format for sessions is to begin with the homework assigned, followed by a discussion of the issues that emerge. During the last 15 minutes of the session, the assignment for the next week is introduced and is accompanied by the necessary explanation, definition(s), and handout.

Homework Assignment 1

Please write at least one page on what it means to you that you were raped. Please consider the effects the rape has had on your beliefs about yourself, your beliefs about others, and your beliefs about the world. Also consider the following topics while writing your answer: safety, trust, power and competence, esteem, and intimacy. Bring this with you to the next session.

Stuck Points: What Are They?

Throughout the rest of therapy we will be talking about stuck points and helping you to identify what yours are. Basically, stuck points are conflicting beliefs or strong negative beliefs that create unpleasant emotions and dysfunctional or unhealthy behavior. Stuck points can be formed in a couple of different ways:

1. Stuck points may be conflicts between prior beliefs and the rape.

   ### Prior Belief

   You can't be raped by someone you know.

   ### Rape

   You are raped by someone you know.

   ### Results

   If you cannot change your previous beliefs to accept what happened to you—that is, that you *can* be raped by someone you know—then you may find yourself asking, "Was it really a rape?"

   If you are asking yourself if it was really a rape, you may be making sense of the rape by saying, "I must have misinterpreted what happened. . . . I didn't make myself clear. . . . I must be crazy or I must have done something to mislead him."

   If you are stuck here, it may take some time until you are able to get your feelings out about the assault.

   ### Goal

   To help you change the prior belief to "You *can* be raped by someone you know." When you are able to do this, you are able to label the event as a rape (accept that it happened) and move on from there.

2. Stuck points may also be formed if you have prior negative beliefs that are confirmed or reinforced by the rape.

Prior Belief

Men are no good.

Rape

You are raped by a man.

Results

If you see the rape as further proof that men are "no good," then you will believe this very strongly.

If you are stuck here, you may have strong emotional reactions that interfere with your ability and desire to have relationships with men. This may feel "safe" to you, but unless this is how you wish to live the rest of your life, it deserves some attention.

Goal

To help you modify your beliefs so that they are not so extreme. For example, "Some men are no good, but this is not true of all men."

5

Session 2:
The Meaning of the Event

The therapist reviews the cognitive formulation of PTSD and depression. Then the therapist reviews and discusses the client's assignment to write about the meaning of the event and begin to look for stuck points—that is, conflicting beliefs or frightening thoughts that interfere with acceptance of the event (complete processing), increase avoidance, or both. (In the first case example below, stuck points evident throughout the initial homework are in italics.) If the client has not done the homework, then the therapist should discuss the importance of completing homework assignments and then ask the client if she thought about the meaning of the event. We never reinforce avoidance. If a client does not do her homework or "forgets to bring it in," we proceed with the assignment during the session. The client should read this and all other assignments out loud. If the therapist were to read it, the client could tune out. It is another attempt at avoidance.

Today we are going to work on identifying what the different feelings are and we will be looking at the connection between your thoughts and feelings. Let's start with some basic emotions—mad, sad, glad, and scared. These four basic emotions can be combined to create other emotions like jealousy (mad plus scared) or can vary in intensity (for example, irritated, angry, or enraged). Can you give me an example of something that makes you mad? ... When do you feel sad? ... How about happy? ... What frightens you? ... How do you feel physically when you are feeling angry? ... How do you feel physically when you are feeling scared? ... How are mad and scared different for you?

The therapist then describes how interpretations of events and self-statements can affect feelings. The therapist can use as an example an acquaintance walking down the street and not saying hello to the client. The client is then asked what she would feel, and then what she just said to herself (for example, "I'm hurt. She must not like me.").

The therapist might ask, "I wonder if someone else might have different thoughts about her behavior?" If the client is unable to generate other alternative statements, the therapist should present several other possible self-statements: "She must not have her glasses on," "I wonder if she is ill?" "She didn't see me," or "What a rude person!" Then the therapist can ask the client what she would feel if she said any of the other statements. It can then be pointed out how different self-statements elicit different emotional reactions.

Now, let's talk about the essay you wrote. What kinds of things did you write about when thinking about what it means to you that you were raped? What feelings did you have as you wrote it?

CASE EXAMPLE 1

One client wrote the following.

The beliefs I had growing up about rape were simple: *Good girls don't get raped; it will never happen to me or I'll fight back and won't allow it; good people don't rape people; people you know or love don't rape you.* When I got married at age 20, he was 19 ½ years old. These same beliefs seemed to continue along with a few more added: *Wives are subservient to their husbands; husbands don't or can't rape their wives; you will or should do anything for your husband in the name of Love!* The effects of the rapes and sexual abuse are many. I started not wanting to go to bed at night with my husband not knowing what to expect, yet afraid to leave him—*"Catholics don't get a divorce."* I hated myself for how he treated me, my self-esteem and self-worth were 6 feet below the gutter. I felt helpless and powerless over the situations. I was afraid to tell a soul; Who would believe me? and what would they think of me for *allowing it to be repeated! I began to trust no one, especially the ones you love who are close to you. I fear any kind of intimacy or closeness even with the ones I love dearly.*

After reading her assignment to the therapist, the client said that she had experienced feelings of anger and hatred. She was angry at herself for letting it happen more than once. She recognized, after reading what she had written, that she had changed because of the rape. The client also stated that she found it helpful to write, that it made her feel better afterward.

The therapist hypothesized that the act of writing about it helped her to accept what had happened and made the event more real. The client agreed. The therapist pointed out that these conflicts between her prior beliefs and the rapes were the stuck points that she would need to be working on, particularly those that left her feeling badly about herself. In this case, the client was able to recognize both her thoughts and feelings so the therapist did not need to probe for her feelings. The therapist reaffirmed the connection between the client's beliefs and her subsequent feelings.

If the client does not recognize her feelings or their connection to her beliefs, help her tie her thoughts to her feelings and behavior. "How do these thoughts influence your mood? . . . How do they affect your behavior?" The therapist should make sure she sees the connection between her thoughts, feelings, and behaviors.

As stated previously, the purpose of this assignment is to have the client examine the impact that the rape has had on her life in several different areas. When reading the essays, it will be important for the therapist to determine whether or not this goal has been achieved. In this next example, the client was able to touch on each area, although she had more difficulty examining the overall impact that this event had on her life. It is evident that this client had difficulty examining these issues in any depth, though clearly she had numerous stuck points to address in therapy.

CASE EXAMPLE 2

> Thoughts!
>   I was violated—I felt powerless—I was confused—Angry! All trust was broken! I learned not to trust early in childhood. As a result, trusting others has always been difficult. Sometimes I don't trust myself.
>   I do not know how to be intimate with anyone—If I start to feel close to anyone I usually end the relationship or they end it for me. I don't like to be controlled. Power at times is frightening to me.
>   Most of my life I have felt a low self-esteem—I have displayed a lot of destructive behavior—mostly to myself! I'm realizing my past has affected my life more than I could have ever imagined. I used to think when bad things happened to me—it was my fault—I deserved it.
>   Crisis has always seemed easier for me than coping with day to day living. My thoughts and actions have always been all or *nothing*—I would like to feel like a whole person and strive toward a balanced way of living.

The first two questions posed by the client in therapy are "Was it really a rape?" and "Why did it happen?" These questions often emerge with the very first homework assignment.

CASE EXAMPLE 3

In this next case, the client stopped reading her meaning statement. The following interchange then occurred.

Client: Why did this have to happen? Why? Why?
Therapist: Why did the rape have to happen?
C: Yeah. Why did he do that to me? Why should I have to feel this? (Long pause.) I'm a product of my environment. I really feel like that.
T: We all are to a certain extent.
C: Yeah. We are.

T: What answer have you given yourself up to this point to that why question? Why did it have to happen? Why do you have to go through this?

C: I guess just that's my life, that was my past. (Laughs.) That is what happened.

T: But you still keep asking why.

C: I think my why question stems from, you know, you stupid son-of-a-bitch, you don't take that from someone. You know, it's not why did he take it from me. One thing I get mad at myself is, (crying) why did I let him?

T (softly): You didn't let him.

C: I know.

T: Did you? He just did it.

C: It happened. I was. . . . I know. I was 15. I was so scared.

T: And confused.

C: Yeah. And alone. I guess that's why it hit me. Because I was so alone. . . . It kind of wiped away all the good memories.

T: It's the scariest thing for a 15-year-old to try to reach out to people when they're feeling bad about themselves. At times a person in that position is going to pull away because she's so afraid of compounding the trauma by other people rejecting her. It seems almost better to walk away yourself than let other people reject you. And to reject them first.

C: Well, for that year afterward I really was mixed up.

T: But you didn't have a label for what happened to you. Did you? You weren't saying, "I have been raped," were you? So even if they had asked, you wouldn't have been able to put it into words that would have been able to express what you had been through.

C: I didn't consider it rape. I didn't know it was. . . . I didn't.

T: You knew it was awful but you didn't have a word for it.

C: I was so ashamed of it. (She starts to read homework assignment again.)

This client had been angry at her parents because she had changed so much after the rape and they did not guess what had happened. Although her parents had always been supportive, she was unable to share this trauma with them, and she withdrew from friends and family for many years. At the end of this session, after further discussion, she realized why she had not told them and understood that they could not have known. It was then that her anger at them dissipated.

Several A-B-C sheets are given to the client (see handout at the end of the chapter).

These homework sheets will help you to see the connection between your thoughts and feelings following events. Anything that happens to you or you think about can be the event to look at. You may be more aware of your feelings than your thoughts at first. If that is the case, go ahead and fill out Column C first. Then go back and decide what the event was (Column A). Then try to recognize what you were saying to yourself (Column B). Try to fill out these sheets as soon after the events as possible. If you wait until the end of the day (or week) you are less likely to remember what you were saying to yourself. Also, the events you record don't have to be negative events. You also have thoughts and feelings about pleasant and neutral events. If you have any memories or thoughts about the rape, please record these also. Don't avoid thinking and writing about the rape.

The client and therapist should fill out one sheet together during the session. As the sample, an event the client has already brought into therapy or some event that occurred within the past few days should be used.

Homework Assignment 2

Please complete the A-B-C sheets to become aware of the connection between events and your thoughts, feelings, and behavior. Use the sheets to record everyday events but also complete at least one sheet on your thoughts about the rape. Remember to fill out the form as soon after an event as possible. Bring these sheets to the next session.

A-B-C Sheet

Date:_____ Client #:_____

ACTIVATING EVENT   BELIEF   CONSEQUENCE

A ———————▶   B ———————▶   C
"Something happens"   "I tell myself something"   "I feel and do something"

Does it make sense to tell yourself "B" above? _____

What can you tell yourself on such occasions in the future? _____

46

6

Session 3: Identification of Thoughts and Feelings

The therapist should begin by going over the A-B-C sheets completed for homework. If the client had difficulty, the therapist should help her identify how her thoughts affect her feelings. The client should try different self-statements in order to modify her affective response. The therapist also looks for stuck points. As an example, one client brought in a sheet in which she had identified the event at "A" as "Taking a shower." At "B" she listed the following thoughts:

Something bad could happen.
I can't hear every sound.
I can't see everything.
I'm isolated.
I can't protect the kids.
I can't protect myself.
Don't relax.
Stay on guard.

Hurry, hurry, hurry.
Don't pull the shower curtain shut all the way.
Bring the knife.

Although this client had been raped in her car, she generalized her fear to the shower. At the time she began therapy, she would take a shower with a knife between her teeth. Under "C" she wrote "Scared—that something bad will happen" and "Angry—because I won't relax and enjoy."

The client was first praised for correctly identifying the event, her thoughts, and feelings. The therapist observed that most of the thoughts listed on this sheet (and her other sheets) appeared to indicate thoughts about her vulnerability to attack. In discussing these thoughts, the client stated that she blamed herself for the rape because she felt she had not been aware enough of her surroundings. She said that if she were attacked again she would blame herself even more; she would feel she was not aware enough to prevent a second attack. This belief was identified as a stuck point for the client.

Frequently, clients label thoughts as feelings. For example, one client brought in an A-B-C sheet that read, "Get yelled at before I even have my coffee" at A, "I try so hard but never get rewarded" at B, and "I feel like I'm fighting an unsuccessful battle" at C. The therapist again labeled the four basic emotions for the client and asked her which of the four feelings fit the statement best. She said, "sad and angry." The therapist pointed out that what she had listed at C was actually another thought that could be listed at B. The client was able to understand the distinction between thoughts and feelings. The therapist also pointed out that just using the words "I feel . . ." in front of a thought does not make that thought a feeling. Clients are encouraged to use the words "I think that . . ." for thoughts and to reserve "I feel" for emotions.

On the next page is an A-B-C sheet as it was completed by clients. At this point in treatment we do not challenge strongly the maladaptive statements we encounter. Some clients are adamant that these statements are true and unchangeable. However, some clients begin to question the validity of their beliefs, and we encourage this examination.

A-B-C Sheet

Date: _____ Client #: _____

ACTIVATING EVENT	BELIEF	CONSEQUENCE
A	**B**	**C**
"Something happens"	"I tell myself something"	"I feel and do something"
I want to read my favorite book. *The man that wrote the book looks just like the man that raped me.*	*Do I want to pick this book up?* *The individual who wrote the book and the man who did the rape are two different people.*	*Cautious and scared.* *I pick up the book and look at it with hatred.*

Does it make sense to tell yourself "B" above? _____Yes_____

What can you tell yourself on such occasions in the future? _Find a different cover for my book or get a different one._

49

The homework for the next week is to write a detailed account of the incident. The client is asked to write down exactly what happened. She should be encouraged to include sensory detail (sights, sounds, smells, and so on) and her thoughts and feelings during the crime. If the client is unable to complete the assignment, she should be encouraged to write as much of it as she can. She may need to write on several occasions to complete the assignment. If she is unable to complete the assignment in one sitting, she should draw a line at the point she stopped. The therapist may be able to determine some of the stuck points by examining the points at which she quit writing. The client should be instructed to read the account to herself at least once before the next session, but preferably every day. If the client has been raped more than once, she should be asked to write about the most traumatic event first.

Encourage the client to pick a time when she has privacy and can cry and feel other emotions without being interrupted or embarrassed. If she has small children who require constant attention, suggest she complete the assignment after the children have been put to bed for the night. Be direct about discouraging completing homework at work during lunch or in a public place. Identify this as avoidance behavior.

The therapist should add the following:

Don't be surprised if you feel your reactions almost as strongly as you did at the time of the incident. Your feelings have been stored in your memory intact. If you have not dealt with this event, your feelings and the details of the event are quite vivid when you finally confront the memory in its entirety. People tend to remember traumatic events in much greater detail than everyday events. Over time, if you continue to allow yourself to feel your feelings about the event, your feelings will become less intense and less overwhelming.

There are two purposes for the writing assignments. The first purpose is to serve as an exposure technique. Writing about the event in great detail assists in calling up the complete schema about the event, including the emotions that have been encoded with the memory. Retrieving the emotions allows them to be fully expressed and dissipated. The memory then can be stored without such intense emotions encoded with it. The second purpose is for the therapist and client together to begin to search for "stuck points," conflicts and cognitions that indicate assimilation or self-blame.

Homework Assignment 3

Please begin this assignment as soon as possible. Write a full account of the rape including as many sensory details (sights, sounds, smells, and so on) as possible. Also include as many of your thoughts and feelings as you recall having during the event. Pick a time and place to write so you have privacy and enough time. Do not stop yourself from feeling your emotions. If you need to stop writing at some point, please draw a line on the paper where you stop. Begin writing again when you can and continue to write the account even if it takes several occasions. Read the whole account to yourself at least once before the session. Allow yourself to feel your feelings. Bring your account to the next session.

7

Session 4: Remembering the Rape

The therapist should begin the session by having the client read the written account. It is important that the therapist allow and encourage the client to express her emotions about the event and help her to identify both her thoughts and feelings. The client should be encouraged to discuss her feelings and thoughts while doing the assignment as well as during the incident: "What was the most frightening part for you?" "Is there some aspect of the incident that you shy away from recalling?"

This exercise may help the client and therapist to identify her stuck points if they have not already been identified. The therapist should notice the points at which the client stopped writing and ask if these were particularly difficult points in her memory and why: "What were you feeling at the time that you quit writing?"

Often these points are particularly anxiety-provoking because they were the most life-threatening to the client or the point at which she perceived a loss of control over the situation and gave up fighting.

In the case example that follows, a 16-year-old client was brought to therapy by her parents 9 months after being raped by a former boyfriend. She had just told her parents about the incident because the assailant began harassing her. At the time she began therapy, she was suicidal and had PTSD. Her written account is as follows:

CASE EXAMPLE 4

It was January 3, 1988. I remember because we went back to school and my friend had left on the second. The weather was warm even though there was a little bit of snow on the ground. That was why my window was unlocked, because I had it open that day. I went to bed around 10:00.

I remember waking up and seeing John on top of me. At first nothing sank in my head of what was happening. After I suddenly realized that he was inside me I froze. I felt paralyzed everywhere. I tried to move my arms and legs but my body wouldn't. It was like my body was just a shell and I was trapped inside, watching it happen with no control. Though my mind was racing, I don't remember what I was thinking. I felt helpless, frightened and couldn't believe John was doing this. It couldn't be me or him. Nothing happened inside me because he pulled out before it did. At this point things are very unclear. I remember pieces. For instance, I remember seeing him sitting on the edge of my bed with his head in his hands. He was saying something like "I can't believe what I just did." My eyes were closed until I heard him open the window and then I saw him jumping out. At that point I closed my eyes and just laid there asking myself "What just happened?" until I fell asleep [dissociated?]. Everything is so unclear. Almost as if I remember but I don't believe it. The next morning I went on with my everyday jobs, as if nothing ever happened.

When this client recounted her story, she did it without any expressed emotion. The account was read word for word without elaboration. She claimed that she simply felt "numb" while doing the assignment, which is not unusual since most of what she was able to recall at the time was a sense of paralysis and disconnectedness from the event. She was unable to recall the most frightening parts of the event, leaving her with only fragments of the entire memory.

This particular account is typical in that it was incomplete at first due to dissociative reactions that occurred during the event. It is also not unusual to get this type of account from clients who are very avoidant. In addition, her initial reported numbness in recounting the event is also common. Over time, as they begin to resolve their cognitive conflicts, most clients are able to recover most of their memories and experience their emotions. Given that this component of therapy is designed to expose the client to the details she has avoided and to allow her feelings to be expressed and extinguished, it is important that the therapist ask the client to continue to write about and relay the event in order to ferret out the most difficult memories and thereby pinpoint stuck points that interfere with adaptive accommodation.

Many of the accounts we have seen are much longer, more graphic, and elicit intense emotions. The therapist needs to be supportive and allow the client to experience her emotions fully without inadvertently cutting them off. Extinction occurs when the emotions are allowed to run their course. Memories of the event can then be encoded and recalled without such strong feelings attached.

Therapists reading or hearing graphic accounts may experience secondary traumatization and may need to process their own reactions to hearing these accounts (McCann & Pearlman, 1990b). If a therapist becomes uncomfortable listening to a client's account of the event, it is possible that the therapist may send subtle signals (and in cases we have heard about, not so subtle signals) to the client that the therapist also cannot handle the event. For example, immediately handing the client a tissue tells the client to pull herself together (and dry up). Shutting the client down is a fatal error on the part of the therapist. In order for the client to be able to accept and integrate the event and tolerate her emotions, the therapist must also be able to do so.

If the client did not do the assignment, the therapist should first ask her why she did not complete it. Discuss the problem of avoidance and how it prevents recovery. Then ask the client to relate the event as if she had written it. Be sure to help the client identify her thoughts and feelings as she recounts the event.

If the client reads or recounts the event without any emotion, the therapist should stop the client and ask her if she is holding back her feelings and why. The therapist may need to discuss the issue of loss of control and the client's fear of being overwhelmed by her emotions ("I will go crazy, forever."). The analogy we typically use is one of a flood. When a flood occurs, the water does not continue forever. There is a rush, but it is temporary and eventually the storm abates, the land dries up, and everything begins to return to normal. Emotions can be viewed the same way. At this point, the therapist can ask the client to recall times when she has experienced feelings such as sadness or anger and what happened after she allowed herself to feel her emotions. It can also be helpful for the therapist to remind her that the actual event, the rape, is over and that she is no longer in imminent danger. The strong feelings are of a memory. After addressing this issue, the therapist should resume with the account and ask the client what she was feeling at the time. When a client begins to experience emotions, it is important that the therapist sit quietly and not disrupt the emotions, minimize them, or interfere in any way.

It is not unusual for the client to report having experienced physiological reactions of sexual arousal during the event. If it is not reported, the therapist should probe for it by stating that it is not unusual for the body to respond physically when stimulated. This is a particularly sensitive issue because if it occurs, the victim often feels that her body has betrayed her, becomes confused about the meaning of the reaction and may feel great shame, making it difficult to discuss or even admit to these reactions. Sometimes women assimilate, or distort the event because of the arousal, and wonder if it was a rape at all. The therapist should explain to the client that physical arousal does not mean that she enjoyed the event or that it was not a rape:

> The clitoris is a bunch of nerve endings that respond when stimulated (like a sneeze). It (the clitoris) doesn't think or make judgments about the situation. A woman's arousal has nothing to do with her worth as a person, her values, or morals. Even if the rapist says something about you enjoying the rape, that doesn't mean that you did. Consider the source of that statement.

With regard to the rapist, the therapist may find it informative to ask the client what he said to her during and after the incident. She may believe what he said without considering the validity of the statements. Because he behaved as if the statements were true, she may have adopted the same viewpoint (or she may have believed the same about rape victims before the event): for example, women who are raped ask for it, are worthless, and only good for one thing, that they were picked because they were behaving in some particular way, and so on. Sometimes during or after the event, the rapist acts in a way that confuses the victim. He tucks her in, kisses her gently goodbye, tells her to lock the door so she will be safe, or engages in some other affectionate behavior. He is obviously distorting the event to himself so that the assault is not a rape in his mind. However, the victim is left confused because his behavior does not match the image of how a rapist "should" behave. She may question whether the event was in fact a rape because she cannot reconcile this behavior with his previous violence and inconsideration. These inconsistencies are often stuck points for the victim.

Finally, the therapist should ask the victim about stuck points that may not be in her written account, such as what she thought she should have done. Most frequently, victims have regrets afterward because they feel they should have prevented it or did not fight hard enough, and some regret that they did not go to the police right away. Sometimes stuck points emerge because other people respond to hearing about the event by second-guessing the victim's behavior: "*I* would have fought harder, gotten away when . . . ," and so on. The therapist may have to discuss 20-20 hindsight and how easy it is to say how you should have behaved after something occurs. This can be a particularly difficult stuck point if the other person's comment mirrors what the victim previously believed about how she would act in such a situation: "If *I* were ever attacked, I'd fight until I died rather than get raped." No one knows how they will respond in a particular situation. Sometimes victims jump to the faulty conclusion that if they had acted differently in some way, the rape would not have occurred. Even if the victim had responded differently, the rapist probably would have acted differently and the event may have occurred anyway (or been more violent).

For homework, the therapist asks the client to start over and write the whole incident again at least one more time. If the client has been unable to complete the assignment the first time, she should be encouraged to write more than last time. Often, the first version reads like a police report with nothing but the facts. The client should be encouraged to add more sensory details as well as more of her thoughts and feelings during the incident. The therapist should add that this week the client is also requested to write her current thoughts and feelings, what she is thinking and feeling as she is writing the account in parentheses (for example, "I'm feeling very angry"). If the client was raped more than once, the therapist should encourage her to begin writing about the other event(s). Also, the trauma may encompass much more than the rape. Police proceedings, the medical examination, the trial, pregnancy or abortion, or rejection from loved ones compound the trauma and should be considered part of the rape for all practical purposes. Memories of these events and concomitant stuck points should be included in the writing assignments and discussions. The client should be reminded to read over the new account at least once, and preferably several more times, before the next session.

Homework Assignment 4

Start over and write the whole incident again at least one more time. If you were unable to complete the assignment the first time, please write more than last time. Often, the first version reads like a police report with nothing but the facts. Add more sensory details as well as your thoughts and feelings during the incident. Also, this time, write your current thoughts and feelings in parentheses (e.g., "I'm feeling very angry"). Remember to read over the new account at least once before the session. If there was a second incident, please begin writing about that event. Bring your written accounts to the next session.

8

Session 5: Identification of Stuck Points

The therapist should begin the session by going over the new version(s) of the incident. The client is helped to analyze her feelings then and now. The client should discuss the differences and similarities between how she felt at the time of the rape and how she felt as she wrote about it. The client should be asked how she felt after writing and reading about the rape a second time as compared to the first time. It is likely that the intensity of emotions will be less the second time if she allowed herself to feel her emotions the first time. The therapist should point out the difference as an example of how the feelings will become less intense over time (or temporarily increased if she managed to avoid her feelings during the first writing assignment).

CASE EXAMPLE 5

This is the first written account of one individually treated client.

I can't remember where I went or what I did on the day of the rape. I can't even remember if it was a weekend or weekday, but I must have come back from studying because my backpack was on the sofa and my notes were on the kitchen table. It was probably close to 5:00 P.M. because it was dusk while we were arguing. I don't think I'd been home very long because I remember hanging up my coat before Mac knocked on the door. He asked for one of my roommates, and when I told him she wasn't here, he came in and wanted to talk. At some point he said she told him I was seeing Joe and that other people had seen me leaving his room so I must be sleeping with him. I think first I told him I wasn't, which was true, and then I thought I shouldn't have to feel I should defend myself. I felt initially guilty. So I got mad and told him it was none of his business. He said if I could sleep with Joe I could sleep with him. I can't remember his next words. He then started to yell that obviously I was fucking everybody in sight and that what's good enough for him is good enough for me. His face was close to mine and I could smell beer but he didn't look drunk (e.g., walked straight, didn't slur words). I told him to get out and tried to push him away. He grabbed both my wrists together and started dragging me down the hallway. It wasn't very far. The apartment was very small and I was afraid. My legs were shaking because I couldn't brace them against the floor. I didn't consciously think he'd rape me, even though it should have been obvious. I guess I thought he'd scare me and then leave. I started crying and tried to kick him. I don't remember if I fell or he pushed me, but my left shoulder was burning like my arm had been pulled out of its socket. I don't remember walking to the bedroom either, so I'm not sure how I actually got there. I was lying on my back with my head scraping against the wall, going the wrong way (sideways) across the bed. I remember I wore a blue denim shirt with no bra, pull-on red sweats with a cream stripe down the middle side of the leg, and was barefoot. It's hard to recall exactly what happened next, except I remember tasting blood on the inside of my lip and tongue. I think I bit it. He twisted my arm and ripped my buttons open and pulled my shirt off but I can't remember my sweats coming off. I also think some time went by before he ripped my shirt off but I don't know why I think that. There was the wall scraping at the back of my head and I had a cramp in my foot, my left arch. If he said something or I did I don't know what it was. It was almost like a picture with no sound to it.

- - - - - - - - - - -

I've only got images, pictures in my head of scenes but not sequences. I didn't have anger and I think I'd stopped crying. I felt absolutely nothing. I felt his penis going in and out of me and my head banging on the wall. I burned so badly, like his penis had needles on it or something. My breasts ached and stung but I don't remember him touching them. He still had my hands together above my head. There's another image that seems separate. I'm not sure why but he was panting hard and his stomach was wobbling and I thought how flabby he was. I remember thinking I would grab the lamp and hit him so he must have let my arms go, but I didn't. The thought wasn't angry or afraid it was like slow motion. Then I remember him leaning in the doorway of my room and the room stank like sweat and semen. He walked around finding his clothes, jeans, boots, blue and white striped shirt, and brown leather jacket. I don't remember moving but after awhile the front door closed. It was so important not to think. I felt all wet under me and inside me and I thought I was going to throw up so I told myself not to think. I still lay there and it was almost dark outside. I don't know how long I was there. I stood at my dresser and I took four Serax. I was very calm but I think I had to lean against the dresser. I wanted to go to sleep but I smelled terrible and I had to be rid of that smell. I didn't think I wanted to kill myself but it was very important that I should go to sleep. I don't remember running the bath water but was lying in it. The tiles were nasty yellow and I thought I'd never have such an ugly bathroom when I got out of school. Sweat was pouring off my head because the water was so hot. I don't remember using soap but my soap in the dish was gone two days later and I had to borrow some from my roommate. I stared at my wrists for a long time. Then my head hit the tub plug on the back of the tub and I thought I'd drown so I got out and almost crawled back to bed. I couldn't get the cover down. The comforter was brown with flowers and he must have raped me on top of the bed because the inside wasn't wet. The room still smelled so I buried my face in the pillow. I woke up because he called and all I remember feeling was irritated because I was still sleepy. He was crying and I think drunk and said, "God I'm so sorry, please say you forgive me. I'd never hurt you. I didn't mean it," or something like that. I said I didn't ever want to talk about it again and hung up. It was dark and I thought it was the same night, only I found out my roommates had tried to wake me up after they found water still in the bathtub. I said I was sick and told them I took something for my stomach that made me sleepy. They said that afternoon I'd told them I was awake but then went back to sleep. I can't remember that either. There was a small amount of blood on the sheets when I got back in bed. I thought if anyone saw it they would just think I started my period. I still felt very calm and very detached but I got dizzy when I was in the shower the next morning and my vagina burned and itched so badly I thought I'd go crazy. I went across the street to the emergency room and the female gynecologist asked me who hurt me and I told her I didn't know what she was talking about and was surprised because I thought she couldn't see my wrists. She said I had bruises on my inner thighs and internal cuts and scrapes and that I shouldn't have bathed. I told her I just had an infection and I wanted to go home. I think she tried to argue some more but the last thing I remember is her handing me three prescriptions and touching my face and said if I changed my mind to call her and she'd write a statement. (I guess for the police). It was almost two years before I told anyone.

The dotted line indicates where the client had to stop writing. She continued writing the account the next day. Although she processed the event fairly quickly, within two sessions, this client continued to be troubled because she could not remember how she got down the hall, even after writing her second account. She was asked to write a third account just focusing on the hallway to try to remember why it was such a stuck point for her. She wrote:

THE HALLWAY

I remember when he started pulling me down the hallway after we had been fighting. He had both of my wrists together and it hurt a lot. He was wearing jeans, a blue and white striped shirt, and boots. He came in with a brown leather jacket but he wasn't wearing it anymore. I was wearing a blue denim shirt, red sweats that had a cream colored stripe, and was barefoot. I felt more vulnerable because I wasn't wearing a bra, but I almost never do when I'm at home. At one time I was irrational enough to think that if I'd been wearing one I might have been O.K.

I was angry and I believe I was still crying and tried to kick him. He dodged and I got his right leg instead and it probably didn't hurt him very much because I was barefoot. Maybe it made him even more angry because I don't remember too much after that. (As I write this and think of it, I start getting heart palpitations and feel nauseated.) I was lying on the floor, half on my side, and my arm and shoulder burned and hurt like it had been pulled out of its socket. I saw his boot and think I must have turned my head and saw the paint chips on the floor in the carpet. My ears were ringing and when I think of it, my ears ring and I don't want to think anymore about it. But it's very important for some reason that he should not have hit me. He might have pushed me and I can't remember getting back up. I saw his feet but I don't remember looking at his face. Anyway, why should I be looking for all the possible reasons why he didn't hit me or push me. I can't remember how I got there or getting back up. I only know that my arm must have been yanked or twisted or both. The carpet felt rough on my face. It's very confusing trying to remember this because I can't tell what my feelings are now and if they are the same or different than how I felt then.

In reading and discussing this account with the therapist, the client suddenly realized why this portion of the event was so traumatic for her. First of all, his violence defined the incident as a rape for her. Second, and more important to her, was that she had been physically abused by her father in childhood. The assailant, her former boyfriend, knew of her father's violence and knew how traumatized she had been by her father's abuse. The boyfriend's violence was to her a major betrayal of the trust she had placed in him to be gentle with her.

An issue that may emerge in one of these two writing sessions may concern the victim's acquaintanceship status with the assailant. Although it will be dealt with in more detail when discussing trust and intimacy in later sessions, it is not unusual for this issue to arise early in therapy. When the woman knows her assailant, she may experience more disbelief and have more difficulty defining the incident as a rape. The client may also express greater self-blame or report more blame or disbelief from others. The client's reactions should be normalized and the therapist should reassure her that acquaintanceship status does not negate the act as a rape.

Self-blame generally is encountered early in therapy as the client recalls the event. It becomes entangled with assimilation because the client, as she writes, looks for ways in which she could have prevented or stopped the rape. This "if only" type thinking serves as assimilation in that it is an attempt to undo the event in retrospect. It usually never occurs to her that the "if only" might not have worked. She assumes it would have worked and feels guilt and shame that she did not behave differently during the rape. She may even conclude that perhaps the event was not a rape because she did not fight hard enough, cooperated at some point with the rapist, and so on.

For example, one client questioned whether the event was a rape because she remembered removing her underpants herself. She ignored the context of coercion and violence in which it occurred.

Another client questioned whether her event was rape because she had been drinking in a bar before being raped by a stranger. Still a third questioned the validity of the crime after recalling that she had placed her hands on the rapist's back while awakening to find the assailant on top of her. The animated discussion that follows clearly illustrates the strong assimilation and self-blame issues commonly found in our groups.

CASE EXAMPLE 6

Client 1: It makes me mad.
Therapist 1: Who are you mad at?
C1: Him.
T1: Yeah. You're mad at him for what?
C1: Because he screwed up my life.
T1: Right.
Client 2: (Crying.) And now I've got to live with this the rest of my life.
C1: (Crying.) It didn't bother me before. Eight years ago. Well, you know, it did, but it didn't. It would come up, and then it's not that bad again . . . shove it back in a drawer. And it's like now . . . I can't. And it makes me mad. And then, like I told Monica, there's a big chunk I don't remember . . . and I don't know if I want to remember. Because there is that block in there that says, "What if I agreed to this?" (Pause.) Did I? And I don't want to . . . because if I find out that I did . . . then it was my fault. You know?
T1: That's people's biggest fear. If you agreed to this, would you be reacting the way you are today? Would any of you?
Client 3: But when you don't have. . . . I totally know what you mean, because I don't remember but probably the last 3 minutes when it was so far gone that I'd already been raped before I even knew what was going on. So when all these things happen to you but you don't remember, you're thinking, I mean the fear of being responsible for putting yourself through this. I don't want to remember it because if I agreed to it, then it is my fault and then all this. . . .
C1: Then I shouldn't be here.
C3: Exactly. Then I don't deserve to be with people who are going through legitimate pain if I don't trust that mine is legitimate. . . .

C1: (Interrupting.) Yes!

C3: When I walk in here, I honestly don't think that my pain is legitimate. I don't. I drove around the parking lot for half an hour rationalizing that I deserve to be here because I sit there and think my pain isn't legitimate. You know, when I'm crying, or when my boyfriend says, "You know, that's terrible. I'm sorry, it's really hard for me to deal with it too," I'm thinking, "Don't give me sympathy because I don't even know if I deserve it." I don't want people's sympathy. But I would take their pity if I felt I deserved it. And sometimes I don't even think I'm good enough to deserve their pity because God knows what happened when I didn't remember. So then I won't take their pity, and torture myself a little bit more because I don't want to remember what happened. Granted, he didn't give me any choices and when I. . . . But what about before when I did have choices? I don't know. When people give me sympathy and compassion I don't feel like I deserve it. It would make me feel a lot better if someone would just say, "Boy, you should have stopped him. That's terrible of you. It's your fault." I would probably feel so much more relieved.

C1: Except I did. And it didn't make me feel better. I did have somebody tell me it was my fault. My husband, to boot.

C2: That happened to me, too. The defense attorney came up and said "You probably walked that way because. . . . "

C1: Well, my husband said, "You left with him"—probably because I was picked up off the floor and slammed up against the wall. He was not to be stood up. You don't stand him up. So my feelings were, "Okay. We'll go and we'll party a little bit and everything will be fine. And I'll go home." But see, I remembered something this week while I was vacuuming . . . that I had forgotten. I remember (crying) taking my pants down. But I remember yelling for him to stop . . . and to get off of me. Then when he threw me back in the car and slammed my head on the steering wheel. . . . It bothered me that I agreed to this.

T1: Did you *agree* to this?

C1: I don't know.

C2: You didn't.

C1: I didn't.

C2: I had to do those things, too. I had a knife to me, but I don't think that's any different.

C1:   Well, I said to Ted (her husband), "You're a guy. What happens if you got involved with a girl and she went along, I mean up to the point of pulling her pants down and the whole bit and then said 'Back off,' would you stop?" He said, "Of course. I might be ticked off, and I might tell her so, but it didn't give him any right to continue."

T1:   Uh-hum. That's right. Say that again, what you just said. It didn't give him a right to continue.   .

C1:   And when we talked about it (she and her husband), when [I told him that] I got sick, and he (the rapist) got off of me so I could throw up, [and then] throw me back in the car, he (her husband) said, "That's not making love." But it's hard for me to agree with because I was the one. . . . I can remember. That scares me. I sat there . . . and did that (pulled her pants off). That's why, like you say, if I agreed to it, it wasn't a rape. I don't deserve to be here.

C3:   My rapist was a friend. He was somebody that. . . . He was a guy, I didn't know him very well. But he's a guy in my class. I was out with friends and I wasn't drunk but I had been drinking. I mean I was just a light-hearted freshman in college. I didn't think to look any deeper into people. I was at a party and he was somebody that was nice and he borrowed my book once. And I was with a big group of people, so I never thought to protect or to be wary. And so, the next thing I know we're at my dorm room and I'm drunk, so I'm in bed, and there's six of us in one dorm room. And so the guy waits until everybody else is asleep and my roommate stayed up until four in the morning, and he waits and then he does it. And then I'm thinking, "Why did I let him in my room?" And I let him walk out. I woke up, he finished what he was doing, and I felt like I was having an out-of-body experience where I was watching it happen to somebody else. And right now talking about it I am completely numb and I don't feel the pain. And then I just let him walk out. And then he tried it again. And then I pressed charges against him. I didn't press charges against him when he actually did the . . . rape. When he came back and he kept, he thought he could do it again, this time he brought a friend. I thought I've got no protection. He picked me and said he can do this, so I thought the only way I can survive is by pressing charges just to get him away from me because he kept hounding me and coming to my door and I wouldn't answer the door. He was my friend! I was thinking, I must be deserving it because he keeps coming back. But at the same time I felt powerless to fight him. I don't know why, but I just felt like . . . I don't know . . . I just stayed away from him. I was sick for a week afterwards—throwing up and everything. You just don't want to believe that somehow you had a part in allowing this to happen to you.

Therapist 2: If it had not been a rape, if it had been a robbery, do you think you would have questioned if it was a robbery or not? If someone had stolen your purse?

C3: No.

T2: It's very different, isn't it? I mean what people tell themselves and what society says, the questions that you got from the attorney you wouldn't have gotten had it been your purse stolen. They wouldn't have said "Why were you there?" and whatever they say that imply blame. And there may have been times during the rape when all of you were in shock and didn't react.

C1: I quit.

T2: There may have been things that you did . . .

C1: (Interrupting.) I shut off. I shut off and said "Obviously, this isn't going to work. So . . . go ahead." That's what I said.

C3: I just said "Do it."

T2: The idea is to get out, still alive, with the least amount of damage. And now that's haunting you because you feel like. . . .

C1: The other thing that makes me mad, because I'm angry at him—I can't remember what he looks like. I can remember the guy who watched over the back seat. I can't remember him. I am just as mad at the guy I can remember, too.

T1: Because he what?

C1: He watched. He didn't help. He didn't stop it.

T1: Right. (Pause.) We can't confuse what happens during the rape with permissive, giving behavior. When people freeze, when people are terrified, frozen, the fight-flight reaction, the majority of people who are raped freeze. Some people fight back. But that doesn't always work, and then they freeze or they just give up and say, "It's not working." The behaviors you do get you through alive. That's why you are all here today.

Client 4: The behavior, too. First of all you get yourself in the situation, it's your fault that you got in the situation. I mean I got in the car with somebody that I worked for.

T2: Is that punishable by rape? That you got in the car with some-body you already knew?

C4: No. But maybe at the time, and maybe after it happened, I really didn't believe that, but then to tell your family. "We told you to never get in the car with. . . . " (Everyone excitedly responds with loud sighs that convey their familiarity with this type of remark.) "So you didn't fight, well that must mean that you wanted it. You were willing. He didn't have a weapon. Well, how much force was there actually? How can you be afraid of somebody who doesn't have a knife or a gun or anything like that?" It's not just your own . . .

T2: Uh-hum. It's what you're hearing from other people.

C4: You come out with some little bit of hope, and then everybody starts putting all of these other things on you and you go, "Hold it, what really happened?"

C3: I let him . . . I mean . . . I put my hands on his back and I just let it happen. I was terrified, but I was more stunned that it was happening. So in a sense, I did let him do it. I put my hands on his back and just laid there. I didn't have too much time, it lasted a good . . . I don't even remember because it was so weird, but it lasted forever. Realistically, it probably didn't last for more than 30 seconds, so he was already doing it before I realized what he was doing. But when I realized . . . I just let him do it. I just put my hand on his back and said, "I'm fucked. This is it, I'm going to lose it after this, but I'm just going to go through with it. I'm not going to take the chance of whatever might happen if I say I'm being raped or if I throw him off." I just thought to myself, "That's it. I'll just take it." I'll take all the repercussions, because I just can't deal with this. There was blood everywhere. I just can't deal with this so I'll just let him do it.

T2: What you did, you did to survive. And that doesn't make it any less of a rape. Not one single bit.

C3: It makes it such a hard reality to deal with because you think in a life-threatening situation you would fight back. Logically, I can think, "well I did that to survive." But it's like a decision I made that's so hard to live with. I saw him all the time because he was on campus.

The list of Challenging Questions (adapted from Beck & Emery, 1985, pp. 196-198) is introduced during this session. The list can be used to question and confront maladaptive self-statements and stuck points (see handout at end of chapter). In order to help clients comprehend the assignment, we have created a handout of a sample that walks the client through the assignment step by step with a stuck point (see handout at the end of the chapter). The therapist should reiterate that stuck points are conflicts between old beliefs and the reality of the rape or negative beliefs that were seemingly confirmed by the rape. The therapist can choose a statement the client has made during the session and use the questions to begin confronting the validity of the belief. At this stage of therapy, it is particularly valuable to focus attention on stuck points indicating assimilation and self-blame. Until the client can accept that she was raped and was not to blame, it will be difficult to work on other issues.

For homework, the client should work on two statements or stuck points by answering each of the questions on the list if they apply. She should write down her answers to bring into the next session. If she has still not finished her written account in detail, she should continue to work on it. If the client has had a second incident and still has not written about it, she should write her account of it as she did with the first incident.

Homework Assignment 5

Please choose two of your stuck points and answer the questions on the Challenging Questions Sheet with regard to each of these stuck points. Write your answers on a separate sheet of paper so that you can keep the list of questions for future reference.

If you have not finished your accounts of the rape(s), please continue to work on them. Read them over before the next session and bring all of your homework to the next session.

CHALLENGING QUESTIONS SHEET

Below are a list of questions to be used in helping you challenge your maladaptive or problematic beliefs. Not all questions will be appropriate for the belief you choose to challenge.

Answer as many questions as you can for the belief you have chosen to challenge below.

Belief:_____

1. What is the evidence for and against this idea?
2. Are you confusing a habit with a fact?
3. Are your interpretations of the situation too far removed from reality to be accurate?
4. Are you thinking in all-or-none terms?
5. Are you using words or phrases that are extreme or exaggerated (for example, always, forever, never, need, should, must, can't, and every time)?
6. Are you taking selected examples out of context?
7. Are you making excuses (for example, I'm not afraid, I just don't want to go out; The other people expect me to be perfect; or I don't want to make the call because I don't have time)?
8. Is the source of information reliable?
9. Are you thinking in terms of certainties instead of probabilities?
10. Are you confusing a low probability with a high probability?
11. Are your judgments based on feelings rather than facts?
12. Are you focusing on irrelevant factors?

Example: Homework 5

CHALLENGING QUESTIONS SHEET

Step 1: Choose a stuck point of yours that creates strong negative feelings or has created changes in your life that you wish to change in some way. Refer back to the sheet on "Stuck Points" that you received in the second session.

Sample stuck point:
Since I went with him voluntarily, it is my fault that I was raped—I should have known better.

Step 2: Go down the 12 questions on the handout and challenge this belief. This is meant to be an exercise in challenging maladaptive thoughts that have created problems for you. The key is that you cannot replace or modify faulty beliefs without knowing yourself *why* they are faulty (that is, the therapist telling you that they are extreme or dysfunctional is not reason enough for you to make changes in your belief system and life).

Remember: Not all questions are appropriate for each stuck point. Here's how it works with the stuck point listed above.

1. What is the evidence for and against this idea?
Evidence for:
I went, so I deserve whatever happened that night (you can even challenge this, too!)
Evidence against:
Just because I went with him it doesn't mean I agreed to have sex with him.
Just because I agreed to go with him doesn't mean he had the right to rape me.
When I went with him I had no idea what he would do to me.
When I went with him all I knew was that he was a nice person.
Going with him didn't mean I caused the rape.
It is impossible to identify a rapist—I could not have known.

2. Are you confusing a habit with a fact?
Here you need to think about whether you have just said this so many times to yourself that it seems like fact or whether it is indeed a fact. A fact is an observable (to others also) provable action or thing.
Yes—I guess just because I went with him voluntarily doesn't automatically mean that I caused the rape.
Maybe because I used to believe this was true of others, I just applied it to myself as if it were fact.

3. Are your interpretations of the situation too far removed from reality to be accurate?
Here you are being asked whether you are distorting what happened in some way, for some reason.
Maybe I am blaming myself more because I am afraid of expressing my anger outwardly or toward the rapist.
I tend to turn things around so it's my fault in general, and it's likely that this is another example of doing that.

I feel as if I have more control over preventing a future rape if I blame something I did in particular than if I blame someone else.

It feels as if I had more control during the rape if I blame myself—I hate to admit that I was totally helpless and out of control of the situation.

It makes me feel safer to think I can identify (and thus should have identified) him as a rapist by something observable, but I know that this is not realistic.

Reality is: It was his fault. He raped me. I did not want this to happen nor did I ask for this to happen. No one deserves to be raped, and no behavior can cause a rape. It is not possible to identify a rapist—by any personal quality.

4. Are you thinking in all-or-none terms?
This also refers to thinking of things as either-or, black-white, right-wrong, good-bad. This belief is more often associated with extreme ways of viewing something with no in-betweens, no grays, no middle ground.
This does not apply to this stuck point.

5. Are you using words or phrases that are extreme or exaggerated (that is, always, forever, never, should, and so on)?
Yes, I think I should have known he would rape me. But I don't know how this is possible.
If I had known he would do this, I would not have gone voluntarily.

6. Are you taking selected examples out of context?
In other words, are you making some judgment without considering the entire context (the whole rape scenario, including what you felt like and thought at the time of the rape and just before)?
Yes, I am taking my voluntarily going with him out of the context of what I expected that night—we were supposed to go out on a date, so it is the norm that a woman will voluntarily leave with a man when they go out.
Another part of this whole scenario is that he gave me signals that he was a nice guy, and he had never in the past done

anything that would have made me suspicious about him (therefore, it makes a lot of sense that I went out with him voluntarily).
This does not mean that I caused the rape or acted in a way that anyone else would not have done.

7. Are you making excuses?
This question is really asking you if you are not being honest with yourself in some way.
This does not apply to this stuck point.

8. Is the source of information reliable?
This question is asking you who the source of the information is and whether they are reliable. This applies best with beliefs originating from what the rapist may have said to you or from blaming comments from other people around you.
Maybe not. So many of my girlfriends and family members have asked me why I went with him—this reinforced my belief that I should have somehow known, since other people implied I should have.
Other people need to believe that they can identify a rapist for their own peace of mind, but they can't; therefore, they are not reliable in their judgment of this event.

9. Are you thinking in terms of certainties instead of probabilities?
This question is meant to challenge stuck points that imply that you are certain that something will happen to you or certainties about people you know or meet.
This does not apply to this stuck point.

10. Are you confusing a low probability with a high probability?
If you answered yes to number 9 above and you realize that you are dealing with a probability, then this question is meant to help you determine whether the probability of X is as high as you think or really much lower.
This does not apply to this stuck point.

11. **Are your judgments based on feelings rather than facts?**
What you want to think about here is whether your stuck point is based on actual fact or your feelings.
Yes, I feel guilty because I think I should have known what would happen, but this is a feeling, and there are no facts to support that it was my fault.
I could not have known this was going to happen. If I can believe this, I will no longer feel the guilt and blame myself.

12. **Are you focusing on irrelevant factors?**
This question is asking you whether or not factors involved in your stuck point (for example, behaviors engaged in, and so on) are relevant to the resulting belief.
Yes—I am focusing on something I did that is in no way connected to the rape—that is, going with him (what I did) did not cause the rape—HE DID!!!

9

Session 6: Challenging Questions

The session begins with the homework and reviewing the client's answers to the questions. The therapist helps the client analyze and confront her stuck points. At this stage of therapy, the most likely stuck points revolve around self-blame for the rape and hindsight as to how it could have been handled differently. The therapist should make sure that underlying attributions, expectations, and other conflicting cognitions have been identified. The relevance of some of the questions that the client was unable to recognize should be pointed out.

As an example, one client had been raped by her hairdresser. She appeared to have a major stuck point regarding her behavior at the end of the incident. She was in conflict because she paid him for the haircut and hugged him upon his request. The stuck point she was working on was "I keep asking myself why I didn't do things different."

In the process of answering the questions, it became clear that the client was ignoring the fact that her behavior that night was based on fear. Now she was feeling angry and was wishing she had been aggressive with him. The therapist helped her to realize that she hugged him and paid him because she was frightened and was trying to get out of the situation as quickly as possible without being injured. When her fear subsided somewhat and her anger emerged later, she could not see that her behavior at the time was understandable. She also did not see that if she had become aggressive, she might have been injured by the rapist. In her fantasies she was victorious, which served to increase her attributions of self-blame about the way she had behaved in reality. The process of answering these questions clarified what this stuck point was and how her thinking had become distorted.

Another client had a similar stuck point she used for the homework assignment. Her repetitive thought had been "I should have been able to stop it." In looking for other ways she could have stopped it, she never found a satisfactory answer, so she kept going in circles. The cycle continued because she didn't stop to question the assumption that she should have been able to stop it. When she stopped and examined the assumption itself with the list of questions, she finally gave up the search for an answer by giving up the question. Her responses to the Challenging Questions are depicted below.

CASE EXAMPLE 7

Challenging Questions Sheet

Below are a list of questions to be used in helping you challenge your maladaptive or problematic beliefs. Not all questions will be appropriate for the belief you choose to challenge. Answer as many questions as you can for the belief you have chosen to challenge below.

Belief: I should have been able to stop it.

1. What is the evidence for and against this idea?
Very little evidence "for"; I didn't have any way of knowing he would do that. I weighed at least 80 pounds less than he

did. I must have been too frozen or too frightened to do anything else, or thought I'd have been hurt worse.

2. Are you confusing a habit with a fact?
To think I ought to have been able to stop it is a habit now, but I don't think it was at first. I think I'm looking for reassurance that it isn't a fact.

3. Are your interpretations of the situation too far removed from reality to be accurate?
I have a hard time separating reality from the way I feel. I don't suppose it's reasonable to expect someone else to have been able to stop it, and I shouldn't do that to myself, either.

4. Are you thinking in all-or-none terms?
Yes—I think if I'd done something more physical to stop the rape that it wouldn't have happened, rather than it might have stopped him.

Another alternative that the therapist pointed out to this client was the possibility that she could have been more seriously hurt or even killed if she had done more than she did at the time.

5. Are you using words or phrases that are extreme or exaggerated (that is, always, forever, never, need, should, must, can't, and every time)?
Yes—should.

6. Are you taking selected examples out of context?
NA

7. Are you making excuses (for example, I'm not afraid, I just don't want to go out; The other people expect me to be perfect; or, I don't want to make the call because I don't have time)?
NA

8. Is the source of information reliable?
No.

9. Are you thinking in terms of certainties instead of probabilities?

See #4.

The therapist discussed this with the client, who was certain that she should have stopped her rapist. She realized, however, that it was more of a probability, a small one at that, that she could have stopped him.

10. **Are you confusing a low probability with a high probability?**
I probably couldn't have stopped him.

11. **Are your judgments based on feelings rather than facts?**
Yes—Guilt, unwillingness to show weakness.

12. **Are you focusing on irrelevant factors?**
I guess stopping it is irrelevant. The point is that it did happen and I can go on with my life.

After discussing the questions, Beck's faulty thinking patterns (exaggerating the meaning of an event, all-or-none thinking, and so on) are introduced. The therapist should describe how these patterns become automatic, creating negative feelings and causing people to engage in self-defeating behavior (for example, avoiding dating because of the conclusion that no man can be trusted). The therapist should use examples from prior sessions or attempt to have the client give an example from a recent event. For homework, the client should consider her stuck points using the handout and find examples for each thinking pattern. She should be asked to look for specific ways in which her reactions to the rape may have been affected by these habitual patterns. In order for clients to understand these faulty thinking patterns better, we give them a sheet with examples along with a blank sheet for them to complete.

Homework Assignment 6

Consider the stuck points you have identified thus far and find examples for each of the faulty thinking patterns listed on the sheet. Look for specific ways in which your reactions to the rape may have been affected by these habitual patterns.

Faulty Thinking Patterns

Below are listed several types of faulty thinking patterns that people use in different life situations. These patterns often become automatic, habitual thoughts that cause us to engage in self-defeating behavior.

Considering your own stuck points, find examples for each of the patterns. Write in the stuck point under the appropriate pattern and describe how it fits that pattern. Think about how that pattern affects you.

1. Drawing conclusions when evidence is lacking or even contradictory.
2. Exaggerating or minimizing the meaning of an event: You blow things way out of proportion or shrink their importance inappropriately.
3. Disregarding important aspects of a situation.
4. Oversimplifying events or beliefs as good/bad, right/wrong.
5. Overgeneralizing from a single incident: You view a negative event as a never-ending pattern of defeat.
6. Mind reading: You assume that people are thinking negatively of you when there is no definite evidence for this.
7. Emotional reasoning: You reason from how you feel.

Examples of Faulty Thinking Patterns

1. Drawing conclusions when evidence is lacking or even contradictory.
Example: All men are untrustworthy.

2. Exaggerating or minimizing the meaning of an event: You blow things way out of proportion or shrink their importance inappropriately.
Example: Since I was not beat up, my rape is not as serious or bad as others I've heard about.

3. Disregarding important aspects of a situation.
Example: Since I did not fight much, it must mean I wanted it.

4. **Oversimplifying events or beliefs as good/bad, right/wrong.**
Example: It was wrong of me not to report the rape to the police.

5. **Overgeneralizing from a single incident: You view a negative event as a never-ending pattern of defeat, or you apply an association you made of the rapist to a whole group.**
Examples: Now that I have been raped, I believe I will be raped again; or All (race, personal characteristics) men are rapists.

6. **Mind reading: You assume that people are thinking negatively of you when there is no definite evidence for this.**
Example: Since my friends and family have not brought up the rape, they must think it's my fault or blame me in some way.

7. **Emotional reasoning: You reason from how you feel.**
Example: Because I feel scared when I am near a man, it must mean that they intend to rape me.

10

Session 7:
Faulty Thinking Patterns

The session should begin with the homework on faulty thinking patterns. The therapist helps the client to confront the automatic self-statements and replace them with other, more adaptive cognitions. Discuss with the client how these patterns may have affected her reactions to the rape (for example, habitually jumping to the conclusion that negative outcomes are her fault may increase the likelihood of self-blame after the assault).

For example, one client was raped as an adolescent. Some male high school friends of hers came to her house and invited her to go for a drive. They indicated that next they would be going over to another female friend's house to pick her up. Instead, they drove the client to the country and gang-raped her. In therapy, her major initial stuck point was that this event was not a rape, because she knew them and went with them voluntarily. She was not even sure that she should be participating in therapy for rape victims. In going over the faulty patterns sheet, she realized that she was drawing conclusions when evidence was lacking and, in this case, even contradictory. She disregarded important aspects of the situation—such as being forced to have sex despite her protests—and she oversimplified her view of herself as being bad and a slut. She also overgeneralized from a single incident, believing men were not trustworthy after the rape. Finally, she decided that rather than exaggerating the meaning of the event, she had, in fact, been trying to minimize it. The therapist agreed.

The therapist pointed out that even if she ignored the situational factors, her level of trauma reaction indicates that the event must have been a rape. If it had not been a rape, she would not have been so traumatized for eight years. The therapist also helped the client to see that if she was forced to have sex against her will, it was rape; the fact that she knew the assailants and went with them voluntarily were irrelevant factors in the definition of rape. Following this intervention, the client expressed some relief to be able to label the event as a rape. Her alternative explanation for her symptoms had been that she was crazy. She now realized that she had been having a normal reaction to a rape.

Below is an actual sample of the faulty thinking pattern homework assignment. It is clear that this woman had both self-blame and safety stuck points to challenge.

CASE EXAMPLE 8

Faulty Thinking Patterns

Below are listed several types of faulty thinking patterns that people use in different life situations. These patterns often become automatic, habitual thoughts that cause us to engage in self-defeating behavior.

Considering your own stuck points, find examples for each of the patterns. Write in the stuck point under the appropriate pattern and describe how it fits that pattern. Think about how that pattern affects you.

1. **Drawing conclusions when evidence is lacking or even contradictory.**

   "I should have been able to stop the rape"—physical size, the inability to physically act or feel, contradict that. But I still think there should have been some unknown way to stop it, and increase the guilt, "responsibility."

   "I'm never safe"—I'm physically safe most of the time, and statistically the likelihood is small that I'll ever be attacked again.

2. **Exaggerating or minimizing the meaning of an event: You blow things way out of proportion or shrink their importance inappropriately.**

   I see an unlocked car or front door, an open window at night and automatically start to react as if it in itself is inherently dangerous, expecting something will happen due to the circumstances.

   I suppose I exaggerate what it means to have not stopped the rape—e.g., I'm responsible, I didn't try hard enough because I couldn't physically injure him.

3. **Disregarding important aspects of a situation.**

   I disregard what would be realistic or even possibly safe for me to have done in stopping the rape; and I overlook the fact that I wouldn't expect someone else to have stopped anything.

   I suppose I disregard what statistics really may mean about the likelihood of my being attacked again.

4. **Oversimplifying events or beliefs as good/bad, right/wrong.**

5. **Overgeneralizing from a single incident: You view a negative event as a never-ending pattern of defeat.**

   I think I overgeneralize from several incidents about something happening to me, and then it doesn't seem like overgeneralization. But I do overgeneralize from "I am not safe in a certain situation" to "I am never safe."

6. **Mind reading: You assume that people are thinking negatively of you when there is no definite evidence for this.**

7. **Emotional reasoning: You reason from how you feel.**

At this point the therapist should introduce the Challenging Beliefs worksheet (adapted from Beck & Emery, 1985, p. 205). Homework will be to analyze stuck points or other rape reactions and to confront and change faulty cognitions. As an example, a stuck point that was identified from the first homework or from preceding sessions should be used. The therapist and client should fill out one sheet together (see handout at the end of the chapter). The therapist should help the client choose at least one stuck point to work on over the next week but also should encourage her to practice by using the sheets for events during the week to which she has emotional reactions.

The therapist should then introduce the first of five specific topics that will be discussed over the next five sessions.

For the next five sessions we will begin considering specific themes that may be areas of beliefs in your life that were affected by the rape. At each session I will be asking you to consider what your beliefs were prior to the rape and to consider how the assault has affected them. If we decide together that any of these themes represent stuck points for you, I will be asking you to complete worksheets on them in order for you to begin changing what you are saying to yourself. The five general themes are safety, trust, power, esteem, and intimacy. Each theme can be considered from two directions: how you view yourself and how you view others.

The first topic we will discuss is safety. If prior to the rape, you thought you were quite safe (that others were not dangerous) and that you could protect yourself, these beliefs are likely to have been disrupted by the rape. On the other hand, if you had prior experiences that left you thinking others were dangerous or likely to harm you, or believing that you were unable to protect yourself, then the rape would serve to confirm or strengthen those beliefs. When you were growing up did you have any experiences that left you believing you were unsafe or at risk? Were you sheltered? Did you believe you were invulnerable to crime?

After the client describes her prior beliefs, the therapist should help her to determine whether her prior beliefs were disrupted or reinforced by the rape. The therapist and client should determine whether she continues to have negative beliefs regarding the

Challenging Beliefs Worksheet

Column A	Column B	Column C
Situation	**Automatic Thoughts**	**Challenging Your Automatic Thoughts**
Describe the event(s), thought(s), or belief(s) leading to the unpleasant emotion(s).	Write automatic thought(s) preceding emotion(s) in Column A. Rate belief in each automatic thought(s) below from 0-100%.	Use the **Challenging Questions** sheet to examine your automatic thought(s) from Column B.
Emotion(s)		
Specify sad, angry, etc., and rate the degree you feel each emotion from 0-100%.		

Adapted from Beck & Emery, 1985.

Column D	Column E	Column F
Faulty Thinking Patterns	**Alternative Thoughts**	**Decatastrophizing**
Use the **Faulty Thinking Patterns** sheet to examine your automatic thought(s) from Column B.	What else can I say instead of Column B? How else can I interpret the event instead of Column B? Rate belief in alternative thought(s) from 0-100%.	What's the worst that could ever <u>realistically</u> happen?
		Even if that happened, what could I do?
		Outcome
		Rerate belief in automatic thought(s) in Column B from 0-100%.
		Specify and rate subsequent emotion(s) from 0-100%.

relative safety of others or her ability to protect herself from harm. They should discuss how negative beliefs can elicit anxiety reactions (for example, "Something bad will happen to me if I go out alone in my car"). The client will need to recognize how these beliefs and emotions affect her behavior (avoidance).

The therapist may need to help the client differentiate prudent safety practices from fear-based avoidance. The client may reduce the probability of being raped through increased safety practices (for example, locking doors) without feeling fearful and panicky or engaging in excessive avoidance behavior. The therapist can point out that the street, parking lot, or nighttime did not rape the client. A particular person who felt like raping at that particular moment in a particular place was the occasion for her assault. Generalized fear is not going to prevent rape and will only serve to prevent recovery.

The therapist should help the client recognize her self-statements and begin to introduce alternative, more moderate, less fear-producing self-statements (for example, replace "I'm sure it's going to happen again" with "It's unlikely to happen again"). Sometimes clients believe that if rape happens once, it will happen again. The therapist may need to give the client some statistics on rape and remind her that rape is not a daily, weekly, or even yearly event for her. It is, in fact, a low probability event. Although the therapist cannot promise that it will not occur again, she or he can help the client to see that she does not have to behave as if it is a high frequency event. The therapist can also point out that the client is jumping to conclusions without supporting evidence.

When this topic comes up, the therapist can say the following:

The rapist owned an hour (or a few hours) of your life. He did have control over that bit of time. Do you want him to continue to own the rest of your life by influencing you to behave differently, as though you are going to be raped at any moment?

The client should be given the safety module to remind her of these issues. The modules on safety and other issues were based on the work of McCann and Pearlman (1990a). If self-safety or other-safety issues are evident in the client's statements or behavior, she should complete at least one worksheet on safety before the next session. Otherwise, the client should be encouraged to complete worksheets on other identified stuck points and recent rape-related events that have been distressing.

Homework Assignment 7

Use the Challenging Beliefs Worksheet to analyze and confront at least one of your stuck points. If you have issues with self- or other-safety, complete at least one worksheet to confront those beliefs. Use the remaining sheets for other stuck points or for recent events that have occurred to you and which have been distressing.

Module 1: Safety Issues

I. Beliefs Related to Self—This is the belief that you can protect yourself from harm and have some control over events.

A. Prior Experience
1. Negative—If you are repeatedly exposed to dangerous and uncontrollable life situations, you may develop negative beliefs about the ability to protect yourself from harm. Rape serves to confirm those beliefs.
2. Positive—If you have positive prior experiences, you may develop the belief that you have control over most events and can protect yourself from harm. Rape causes disruption in this belief.

B. Symptoms Associated with Negative Self-Safety Beliefs
1. Chronic and persistent anxiety
2. Intrusive thoughts about themes of danger
3. Irritability
4. Startle responses or physical arousal
5. Intense fears related to future victimization

C. Resolution
1. If you previously believed that "It can't happen to me," you will need to resolve the conflict between this belief and the victimization experience. Possible self-statement may be "It is unlikely to happen again, but the possibility exists."
2. If you previously believed that "I can control what happens to me and can protect myself from any harm," you will need to resolve the conflict between prior beliefs and the victimization experience. Possible self-statement may be "I do not have control over everything that happens to me, but I can take precautions to reduce the possibility of future victimization."
3. If you previously believed that you had no control over events and could not protect yourself, the rape will confirm these beliefs. New beliefs must be developed that mirror reality and serve to increase your belief about your control and ability to protect yourself. A self-statement may be "I do have some control over events, and I can take steps to protect myself from harm. I cannot control the behavior of other people, but I can take steps to reduce the possibility that I will be in a situation in which my control is taken from me."

II. Beliefs Related to Others—The belief about the dangerousness of other people and expectancies about the intent of others to cause harm, injury, or loss.

A. Prior Experience
1. Negative—If you experienced people as dangerous in early life or you believed it as a cultural norm, the rape will confirm these beliefs.
2. Positive—If you did not experience others as dangerous in early life or you never experienced harm from others and therefore never expected harm from others, the rape will disrupt these beliefs.

B. Symptoms Associated With Negative Other-Safety Beliefs
1. Avoidant or phobic responses
2. Social withdrawal

C. Resolution
1. If you previously believed "Others are out to harm me and can be expected to cause harm, injury, or loss," you will need to adopt new beliefs in order for you to be able to continue to feel comfortable with people you know and to be able to enter into new relationships with others. A possible self-statement would be "There are some people out there who are dangerous, but not everyone is out to harm me in some way."
2. If you previously believed that "I will not be hurt by others," you will need to resolve the conflict between this belief and the victimization. A possible self-statement would be "There may be some people who wish to harm others, but it is unrealistic to expect that everyone I meet will want to harm me."

11

Session 8: Safety Issues

The therapist should begin the session by going over the worksheets and discussing the client's success or problems in changing cognitions. The therapist and client should use the list of questions to help the client confront faulty cognitions that she was unable to modify herself.

For example, one client was accosted by a stranger while sitting in her car in a parking lot as she waited for her husband. The assailant forced his way in at gunpoint, covered her eyes, drove her around, and then raped her. During the rape, the assailant fired the gun next to her head, rendering her temporarily deafened. The client had major issues with safety and felt that she could not go out in her car alone at night.

When she completed the worksheet on the issue of going out (see box on page 92-93), she said that her emotion was fear (90%) and that her automatic thought was that "Something bad might happen," which she believed completely (100%). Under Column C (Challenging Your Automatic Thoughts), she responded that the evidence was that "Something did happen—I got raped." She also wrote that this was logical to her. She wrote nothing in Column D (Faulty Thinking Patterns). In Column E (Alternative Thoughts), she wrote "I could stay home." Under Column F (Decatastrophizing), she wrote "I could be raped again. . . . It would kill me." As an outcome, she re-rated her belief in the automatic thought as 100% and her fear as 90%.

Unfortunately, the above example is often typical of the forms filled out for the first time by clients. The clients are usually so entrenched in their beliefs that they cannot look at them any other way. For this client (and for many who have safety issues), the therapist began to focus on the probability of being raped again. Many women need to become more educated about the probabilities of an individual woman being raped at any particular time. The statistics people are usually given are that 1 out of 4 women is raped, that a rape occurs once every 6 minutes in the United States, and so on. These types of statistics are quite frightening to the victims. The therapist needs to remind the victim that rape is a very low probability event in day-to-day living, and yet she is behaving as if the probability were extremely high. For example, in the case above, the therapist asked the client how much she used to go out and was told that she went out approximately twice a week. The therapist asked her how many times she had been raped or victimized in other ways. The client told her that she had been robbed once about 10 years earlier. At that point, the therapist said:

Okay, you went out about 100 times a year, that's about 1,000 times over the last 10 years. For you, that means that if everything stayed the same and these events occurred at the same rate, and you went out tonight, you might have a 1 in 1,000 chance of being raped and a 999 out of 1,000 chance of not being raped. Does it make sense to you that you walk around being terrified all of the time? The rapist owned three hours of your life and we can't change that. Do you want him to own the rest of your life and to dictate what you can and cannot do?

The therapist also pointed out that the client probably had a greater chance of being in a car accident, yet she did not avoid driving at other times and was not in perpetual fear of an accident. The client agreed with the statements and began to rethink her beliefs. The client

Challenging Beliefs Worksheet

Column A	Column B	Column C
Situation	**Automatic Thoughts**	**Challenging Your Automatic Thoughts**
Describe the event(s), thought(s), or belief(s) leading to the unpleasant emotion(s).	Write automatic thought(s) preceding emotion(s) in Column A. Rate belief in each automatic thought(s) below from 0-100%.	Use the **Challenging Questions** sheet to examine your automatic thought(s) from Column B.
I cannot go out in my car alone at night.	*Something bad might happen.*	*Evidence - Something did happen - I got raped.*
Emotion(s)		
Specify sad, angry, etc., and rate the degree you feel each emotion from 0-100%. *Scared - 90%*		

Adapted from Beck & Emery, 1985.

Column D	Column E	Column F
Faulty Thinking Patterns	**Alternative Thoughts**	**Decatastrophizing**
Use the **Faulty Thinking Patterns** sheet to examine your automatic thought(s) from Column	What else can I say instead of Column B? How else can I interpret the event instead of Column B? Rate belief in alternative thought(s) from 0-100%.	What's the worst that could ever realistically happen? *I could be raped again.*
	I could stay home.	Even if that happened, what could I do? *It would kill me.*
		Outcome
		Rerate belief in automatic thought(s) in Column B from 0-100%. *100%*
		Specify and rate subsequent emotion(s) from 0-100%. *Fear - 90%*

and therapist completed the worksheet a second time. Under Column C (Challenging Your Automatic Thoughts), they wrote "Confusing a low probability for a high probability event." Under Column D (Faulty Thinking Patterns), they wrote "Jumping to conclusions and either/or thinking." She re-rated her fear as 40%. The next week she reported that she had gone out one evening and was not as fearful.

During the remainder of the session, the therapist should introduce and discuss the theme of trust (self-trust and trust of others).

Self-trust is concerned with the belief that one can trust or rely upon one's own perceptions or judgments. After being raped, many women begin to second-guess themselves and to question their own judgment about being in the situation that led to the rape or about their ability to judge character if the rapist was an acquaintance. Trust in others is also frequently disrupted following rape. Sometimes women may feel betrayed by the man who raped them. Also, sometimes women feel betrayed by the people they turned to for support after the rape. Prior to the rape, how did you feel about your own judgment? Did you trust other people? How did your prior life experiences affect your feelings of trust? How did the rape affect your feelings of trust in yourself or others?

The therapist and client should briefly go over the module on trust. For homework, the client should analyze and confront themes of safety and trust using the worksheets.

Homework Assignment 8

Use the Challenging Beliefs worksheets to continue analyzing your stuck points. Focus some attention on issues of self- or other-trust as well as safety if these remain important stuck points for you.

Module 2: Trust Issues

I. Beliefs Related to Self—The belief that one can trust or rely upon one's own perceptions or judgments. This belief is an important part of self-concept and serves an important self-protection function.

A. Prior Experience
1. Negative—If you had prior experiences where you were blamed for negative events, you may develop negative beliefs about your ability to make decisions or judgments about situations or people. Rape serves to confirm these beliefs.
2. Positive—If you had prior experiences that lead you to believe that you had perfect judgment, the rape may disrupt this belief.

B. Symptoms Associated with Post-Assault Negative Self-Beliefs
1. Feelings of self-betrayal
2. Anxiety
3. Confusion
4. Overcautious
5. Inability to make decisions
6. Self-doubt and excessive self-criticism

C. Resolution
1. If you previously believed you could not rely on your own perceptions or judgments, the rape may have reinforced your belief that "I cannot trust my judgment" or "I have bad judgment." In order to come to understand that the rape was not your fault and that your judgment did not cause the rape, you need to adopt more adaptive beliefs. Possible self-statements may be:
   I can still trust my good judgment even though it is not perfect. Even if I misjudged this person or situation, I realize that I cannot always realistically predict what others will do or whether a situation may turn out as I expect it to.
2. If you previously believed that you had perfect judgment, the rape may shatter this belief. New beliefs need to reflect the possibility that you can make mistakes, but still have good judgment. Possible self-statements are: "No one has perfect judgment. I did the best I could in an unpredictable situation, and I can still trust my ability to make decisions, even though it's not perfect."

II. Beliefs Related to Others—Trust is the belief that the promises of other people or groups with regard to future behavior can be relied upon. One of the earliest tasks of childhood development is trust versus mistrust. A person needs to learn a healthy balance of trust and mistrust and when each is appropriate.

A. Prior Experience
1. Negative—If you were betrayed in early life, you may have developed the generalized belief that "No one can be trusted." Rape serves to confirm this belief, especially if the assailant was an acquaintance.
2. If you had particularly good experiences growing up, you may have developed the belief that "All people can be trusted." Rape shatters this belief.

B. Post-Rape Experience—If the people you knew and trusted were blaming, distant, or unsupportive after the rape, your belief in their trustworthiness may have been shattered.

C. Symptoms Associated With Negative Other-Trust Beliefs
1. Pervasive sense or disillusionment and disappointment in others
2. Fear of betrayal or abandonment
3. Anger and rage at betrayers
4. If repeatedly betrayed, negative beliefs may become so rigid that even people who are trustworthy may be viewed with suspicion.
5. Close relationships, particularly when trust is beginning to develop, activate anxiety and terror of being betrayed.
6. Fleeing from relationships

D. Resolution
1. If you had the prior belief that "No one can be trusted," which was confirmed by the rape, you need to adopt new beliefs that will allow you to enter into new relationships with others instead of withdrawing because you believe others to be untrustworthy. A possible resolution may be "Although I may find some people to be untrustworthy, I cannot assume that everyone is that way." Additional resolutions include: "Trust is not an all-or-none concept. Some may be more trust-

worthy than others. Trusting another involves some risk, but I can protect myself by developing trust slowly and including what I learn about that person as I get to know him or her."

2. If you grew up believing that "Everyone can be trusted," the rape will shatter this belief. In order to avoid becoming suspicious of the trustworthiness of others, including those you used to trust, you will need to understand that trust is not either-or. "I may not be able to trust everyone, but that doesn't mean I have to stop trusting the people I used to trust."

3. If your beliefs about the trustworthiness of your support system were shattered, it will be necessary to address general issues before you assume that you can no longer trust them. Of central importance is to consider their reaction and the reasons why they may have reacted in an unsupportive fashion. Many people simply do not know how to respond and may be reacting out of ignorance. Some respond out of fear or denial because what has happened to you makes them feel vulnerable and may shatter their beliefs. Practicing how to ask for what you need from them may be a step to take in assessing their trustworthiness. If your attempts to discuss the rape with them leaves you feeling unsupported, you may resolve the conflict by adopting the belief that "There may be some people I cannot trust talking with about the rape, but they can be trusted to support me in other areas." If such a person continues to blame you and make negative judgments about you, you may decide that this person is no longer trustworthy. It is unfortunate, but sometimes you find out that some people you thought of as friends do not turn out to be true friends after a victimization. However, you may also be pleasantly surprised to find that some people have better reactions than you expected.

12

Session 9: Trust Issues

As with the other sessions, the therapist should begin by going over
the homework and discussing the client's success or difficulties in
changing cognitions. Although trust is often an issue for rape victims generally, it is particularly an issue for those who were raped
by acquaintances. Women who are raped by someone they know and
thought they could trust feel especially betrayed and begin to doubt
their own judgment. They often think that they should have been
able to tell that this person could harm them and, as a result, they
begin to question their judgment in who they can or cannot trust.
Looking back at the rape, many women look for clues and indicators
that may have indicated that this event was going to happen. They
judge themselves as having failed at preventing what they decide
was a preventable event.

Self-distrust may even generalize to other areas of functioning,
and the client may have difficulty making everyday decisions. Rather
than falling on a continuum, trust becomes an either-or concept in
which people tend not to be trusted unless there is overwhelming

evidence to the contrary. As a result, they tend to avoid becoming involved in relationships, and some do not date for years. These women not only have trouble trusting men, but also may have difficulty trusting women because of other women's reactions to their having been raped.

The therapist needs to present the idea that trust falls on a continuum and that developing trust in another person takes time as one obtains more information about the behavior of the other person. The therapist can have the client examine the actual behavior of other people rather than just rely on her global judgment that people cannot be trusted. The therapist should empathize that taking the risk to begin to trust another person is frightening for the client but that she can take safety precautions while she develops relationships. For example, the client initially can meet the other person at public places and drive separately. She should set boundaries assertively regarding the amount of physical contact. The reaction of the other person can be important information for the client in determining how well this person respects her and can be trusted. It may be helpful at this point to take a few minutes to define and give examples of passive, aggressive, and assertive behavior and to encourage assertive behavior as the ideal to strive for. (See completed trust worksheet on page 100-101.)

With regard to trusting family and friends, it may be helpful for the therapist to explain why other people sometimes react negatively to the victim: It is a defense against their own feelings of helplessness and vulnerability. Sometimes other people react negatively or withdraw because they simply do not know how to react or what to say, and the victim interprets their reactions as rejection. The therapist can discuss with the client how to ask for the support she needs from others (for example, "I don't need advice or answers from you; I just need you to listen and understand what I am going through").

With regard to self-trust, it is important for the therapist to point out that it is probable that other people would not have picked up on cues that the rape was going to occur either and that no one expects to be attacked by someone they know. In addition, while 20-20 hindsight may be more accurate, no one has perfect judgment about how other people are going to behave in the future. Even if she missed

Challenging Beliefs Worksheet

Column A	Column B	Column C
Situation	Automatic Thoughts	Challenging Your Automatic Thoughts
Describe the event(s), thought(s), or belief(s) leading to the unpleasant emotion(s).	Write automatic thought(s) preceding emotion(s) in Column A. Rate belief in each automatic thought(s) below from 0-100%.	Use the **Challenging Questions** sheet to examine your automatic thought(s) from Column B.
Trustworthiness of people close to me.	*Anyone can hurt me. I cannot trust anyone.* *100%*	*It is true that anyone can hurt me, and even though I may not be able to trust everyone, that doesn't mean I have to stop trusting the people I used to trust.*
Emotion(s) Specify sad, angry, etc., and rate the degree you feel each emotion from 0-100%. *Sad - 80%* *Angry - 20%*		

Adapted from Beck & Emery, 1985.

Column D	Column E	Column F
Faulty Thinking Patterns	**Alternative Thoughts**	**Decatastrophizing**
Use the **Faulty Thinking Patterns** sheet to examine your automatic thought(s) from Column B.	What else can I say instead of Column B? How else can I interpret the event instead of Column B? Rate belief in alternative thought(s) from 0-100%.	What's the worst that could ever <u>realistically</u> happen? *Being hurt by someone abusing his/her trust.*
Mind reading - I prejudged everyone. *Exaggerating the meaning - I could not trust some people, but some I could have trusted.*	*It is easier to trust others once I started trusting myself and my judgment.* *I will always be a little skeptical of people in general, but there will be people I can trust.*	Even if that happened, what could I do? *Stay focused. I cannot control other people. Hold my head up and stay proud of who I am.*
		Outcome
		Rerate belief in automatic thought(s) in Column B from 0-100%. *0%*
		Specify and rate subsequent emotion(s) from 0-100%. *Sad - 20%* *Angry - 5%* *Happy - 75%*

some indicators that the assailant was violent, that does not mean she should be blamed or blame herself for the rape. Acquaintance rape is a betrayal of trust, and the other person is responsible for that betrayal. There are no good predictors of rape and who is going to rape. Many rapists appear quite charming and have a great ability to appear trustworthy. However, in being overly suspicious of everyone, the client may lose many people who are, in fact, trustworthy. In the end, she will only feel isolated and alienated from people who could provide genuine support and intimacy.

The theme of power and control is introduced next as the topic for the next session. The client is given the module on power to read and work with for the next session. Self-power (self-efficacy) refers to a person's expectations that she can solve problems and meet new challenges. Because the rape was out of their control, women who have been raped often attempt complete control over other situations and their emotions. These women may adopt the unrealistic belief that they must control everything or they will be completely out of control. Again, there is a tendency to engage in either-or thinking.

Power with regard to others involves the belief that one can or cannot control future outcomes in interpersonal relationships. Many women attempt to have complete control in any new relationships they may develop after the rape and have difficulty allowing the other member to have any control. As a result, previously existing relationships may become disrupted, or they may have great difficulty establishing new relationships and possibly avoid the situation altogether. This issue is usually closely tied to trust of others and should be explored for stuck points.

The therapist should describe how prior experience affects these schemata and how rape can confirm negative or disrupt positive beliefs. For homework, the client should continue using worksheets to analyze and confront these beliefs.

Homework Assignment 9

Use the worksheets as before to continue to address your stuck points. Complete worksheets on power and competence (self and others).

Module 3: Power Issues

I. Beliefs Related to Self —The belief or expectation that you can solve problems and meet challenges. Power is associated with your capacity for self-growth.

A. Prior Experience
1. Negative—If you grew up experiencing inescapable, negative events, you may develop the belief that you cannot control events or solve problems even if they are controllable or solvable. This is learned helplessness. Because rape is an event over which you had no control at the time, it probably confirmed prior helplessness beliefs.
2. Positive—If you grew up believing that you had control over events and could solve problems (possibly unrealistically positive beliefs), the rape will disrupt those beliefs.
3. Negative beliefs resulting from rape—Negative beliefs are exhibited as unrealistically high or unrealistically low expectancies for personal power.
   a. The belief that one must be in control of oneself, one's emotions, and actions at all times and that any sign of vulnerability represents a sign of weakness and powerlessness.
   b. The belief that one is helpless to control forces both within and outside of the self.

B. Symptoms Associated With Overcontrol or Helplessness
1. Numbing of feelings
2. Avoidance of emotions
3. Chronic passivity
4. Hopelessness and depression
5. Self-destructive patterns
6. Outrage when faced with events that are out of your control or people who do not behave as you would like

C. Resolution
1. Resolution for overcontrol will involve understanding that no one can have complete control over their emotions or behavior at all times. And, while you may influence them, it is impossible to control all external events or the behavior of

other people. Neither of these facts represent signs of weakness, only an understanding that you are human and can admit that you are not in total control of everything that happens to you or your reactions. A possible self-statement is, "I do not have total control over my reactions, other people, or events at all times. I am not powerless however, to have some control over my reactions to events or to influence the behavior of others or the outcome of some events."

2. Resolution for helpless beliefs—In order to regain a sense of control and decrease the accompanying symptoms of depression and loss of self-esteem that often go along with believing you are helpless, you will need to reconsider the controllability of events. A possible self-statement is, "I cannot control all events outside of myself, but I do have some control over what happens to me and my reactions to events."

II. Beliefs Related to Others—The belief that you can control future outcomes in interpersonal relationships or that you have some power, even in relation to powerful others.

A. Prior Experience
1. Negative—If you had prior experiences with others that led you to believe that you had no control in your relationships with others or that you had no power in relation to powerful others, the rape will seem to confirm those beliefs.
2. Positive—If you had prior positive experiences in your relationships with others and in relation to powerful others, you may have come to believe that you could influence others in ways that you chose. The rape may shatter this belief because you were unable to exert enough control, despite your best efforts, to prevent the rape.

B. Resulting Negative Beliefs—Negative power beliefs involve the belief that one must be in control in all relationships or, in contrast, that one has no power and is at the mercy of others. If negative helpless beliefs become fixed, the person is vulnerable to future exploitation or victimization.

C. Symptoms of Faulty Power Beliefs
1. Passivity
2. Submissiveness
3. Lack of assertiveness that can generalize to all relationships.
4. Inability to maintain relationships because you do not allow the other person to exert any control in the relationship (including becoming enraged if the other person tries to exert even a minimal amount of control).

D. Resolution
1. Powerlessness—In order for you to avoid being abused in relationships because you do not exert any control, you will need to learn adaptive, balanced beliefs about your influence on other people. A possible self-statement is, "Even though I cannot always get everything I want in a relationship, I do have the ability to influence others by standing up for my right to ask for what I want."
2. Overcontrol—It is important to realize that healthy relationships involve sharing power and control. Relationships in which one person has all the power tend to be abusive (even if you are the one with all the power). A possible self-statement is, "Even though I may not get everything I want or need out of a relationship, I can assert myself and ask for it. A good relationship is one in which power is balanced between both people. If I am not allowed any control, I can exert my control in this relationship by ending it if necessary."

13

Session 10:
Power and Control Issues

The session should begin with a discussion of the client's attempts to change cognitions regarding power. The therapist needs to help the client regain a balanced view of power and control. Realistically, no one has complete control over all events that occur to them or over the behavior of other people. On the other hand, people are not completely helpless. They can influence the course of events, and they can control their own reactions to those events (see completed control worksheet on pages 108-109).

For example, one client had come to believe that she was helpless and incompetent in many areas of her life because of her helplessness during the rape. As a result of feeling incompetent, she did not assert herself when she had the opportunity. She felt that such efforts would be futile. She felt stuck in a job that was unsatisfying and helpless to influence her employer's unreasonable demands. When the therapist began to help her look at her options, she began to see that she was not totally helpless. As she began to apply and get interviews for other jobs, she felt more comfortable asserting herself with her boss. Although she eventually left that job for a better one, her last months on the first job were more satisfying, and she was able to see that she could effect change in other people.

Another client believed that she was completely in or completely out of control. Her automatic thought was, "If I'm not in control, who is? I can't decide anything if I'm not in control and I don't have a choice in the matter if someone else is controlling the situation." In this case, it was necessary for the therapist to help the client view control as falling on a continuum. The client's alternative thought was, "I can try to change the situation so I do have some control."

The topic of anger frequently emerges in treatment with rape victims. Although many rape victims report that they did not experience anger during the assault, many find that feelings of anger emerge in the aftermath, feelings that they are often afraid to express. They often assume that the expression of anger will result in behavioral aggression. Women in our society are often discouraged from experiencing anger and are therefore inexperienced with its expression. They fear losing control if they allow themselves to feel their anger. One woman in treatment expressed the fear that if she allowed herself to feel anger, it would make her just like the rapist. Women who have been raped need to have their anger validated as a legitimate reaction to having their power and control taken from them during the rape. They need to learn that they can feel their anger, talk about it, or write about it and that they need not become aggressive.

Anger directed at self often emerges as women dwell on all of the things they "should" have done to prevent the rape or defend themselves. Many of the women entering therapy are angry at themselves for this reason. Once they are able to see that a change in their behavior may not have prevented the rape, they may find that they instead become angry at the rapist for taking away their control and creating feelings of helplessness. A certain amount of anger is also directed at society for not making rape a more frequently and severely punished crime.

One woman in therapy expressed anger at herself because she felt she was not competent to deal with the rape. In this case, rather than directing her anger at the rapist for having taken her power, her stuck point was that she should have been able to recover from this

Challenging Beliefs Worksheet

Column A	Column B	Column C
Situation	Automatic Thoughts	Challenging Your Automatic Thoughts
Describe the event(s), thought(s), or belief(s) leading to the unpleasant emotion(s).	Write automatic thought(s) preceding emotion(s) in Column A. Rate belief in each automatic thought(s) below from 0-100%.	Use the **Challenging Questions** sheet to examine your automatic thought(s) from Column B.
I am supposed to have control over myself all the time, at least in front of other people.	*If other people see me crying or screaming, they'll think I'm weak or "crazy."* 75%	*Was told all my life "there's nothing to cry about" and people got angry if I cried.* *The information isn't reliable since it came from an alcoholic and a passive woman who couldn't let herself cry either.* *All-or-none - People may just think I'm sad or angry.* *Exaggerated - Crazy* *Thinking of certainties and high probabilities.*
Emotion(s)		*Based on feelings instead of facts - I haven't allowed myself the risk of getting facts to refute my beliefs.*
Specify sad, angry, etc., and rate the degree you feel each emotion from 0-100%. *Frightened - 90%*		

Adapted from Beck & Emery, 1985.

Column D	Column E	Column F
Faulty Thinking Patterns	**Alternative Thoughts**	**Decatastrophizing**
Use the **Faulty Thinking Patterns** sheet to examine your automatic thought(s) from Column B.	What else can I say instead of Column B? How else can I interpret the event instead of Column B? Rate belief in alternative thought(s) from 0-100%.	What's the worst that could ever realistically happen? *I could lose control and not be able to stop crying or screaming in public.*
Drawing conclusions about what others will think when I haven't allowed myself to find out. *Exaggerating an event - Few people think others who cry or scream are crazy or weak.* *Disregarding aspects - My family wasn't healthy and just because they thought something doesn't make it true. It's not bad or wrong to show vulnerability.*	*Crying or screaming might show I'm human. There are certain situations that it might be better if I didn't, but it doesn't mean I'm "weak" or "crazy."* *Not having total control all the time might provide some release for my pent-up emotions.* *65%*	Even if that happened, what could I do? *I would eventually calm down and ask for some understanding. I could also try to find enough releases so my emotions wouldn't explode.* Outcome Rerate belief in automatic thought(s) in Column B from 0-100%. *40%* Specify and rate subsequent emotion(s) from 0-100%. *Frightened - 45%*

event quickly and by herself. She began to question her competence in many areas of her life. In this case, the therapist needed to remind the victim that most women have difficulties following rape and that some events in life are too big to be handled all alone.

A college-aged woman came in for treatment following two date rapes in a 2-year period. Because she did not label these incidents as rape, she had no way of understanding her trauma reactions. Her self-esteem plummeted. When someone else finally labeled her experiences as rape, she sought therapy. It became evident fairly quickly that this young woman had a great deal of difficulty asserting herself in interpersonal situations. She was raised to be nice to everyone and did not want to be perceived as "mean," so she ended up being taken advantage of in many situations. This became quite clear to her as she began working on Challenging Beliefs worksheets.

At one session she came in with a sheet regarding a situation that had occurred the preceding day. She received a letter in the mail that she had won one of several "valuable" prizes. Although she usually ignored such letters, this time she decided to call out of curiosity. The man who responded to her phone call was quite persuasive about her prize and said she could pay for the $475 water filter he was selling out of her prize money. As the phone call progressed, she became more and more frightened as the man failed to acknowledge her refusal. She finally balked when he asked for her credit card number and put him off by saying that she did not have it because she was in the process of moving. She told him to call back when she knew she would not be there. Upon returning, she found two messages from him and became even more frightened.

After completing a worksheet, she recognized the parallel between this situation and the rapes. He would not take no for an answer and she felt helpless to stop him. In the case example below, you will find the dialogue that occurred between the client and her therapist after the client described the situation and her worksheet.

CASE EXAMPLE 9

Client: It was a weird parallel. I remember thinking, "How am I going to get out of this?"

Therapist: How did you work it through? You said it still is scaring you?

C: It still is a little bit. Actually, I put my outcome rating as 20% as far as my beliefs and feelings, but it still is probably a little higher than that. I don't know why. Realistically, I know—I mean, I know he's not going to come to St. Louis and kill me or something. (Laughs.) But it's weird, I have these really strange fears. I don't know if I watch too many movies about phone callers. I don't know what it is. It's like a really irrational fear, and it's only from knowing that it's irrational that I know that I can deal with it. I can think, "I know it's just irrational, nothing is going to happen, so just forget about it."

T: For the next session I want you to work on a sheet which is "I can't say no."

C: Um, yeah.

T: I want you to work on that one some more.

C: Okay. See here (pointing to column on worksheet)—I said "fear of saying no and not being able to control situation," and then that leads to fear of threats. I was kind of afraid to play my answering machine last night. I don't know why. It's weird.

T: There are going to be other situations; persuasive salespeople are around and persuasive men are around.

C: Yeah, I know.

T: That is one thing you're going to have to learn to do. How to say "yes" when you want to say "yes," and how to say "no" when you want to say "no."

C: Um, yeah.

T: And how you can forcefully say "no" so that they know that "no" means "NO." And not freaking and panicking.

C: (Laughs weakly.) Yeah. That is a big deal. It's strange, too. I just think it's strange that so many people act like, you know, "Gosh, how can you even question that. Just say No! Just hang up!" I don't know why I just couldn't hang up. I mean, it's like I felt that it was mean. And I don't know why I'm so worried about being mean to someone I've never met and am never going to meet. And it doesn't matter, and he's making me uncomfortable.

T: Was there a component of that in the rapes?

C: Yeah.

T: Where you didn't want to be mean and didn't want to scream and call attention to yourself?

C: Totally. That was a very big factor. I mean I kept hoping it would
just stop so I could just get out without any incident. I was
thinking if I was more quiet about it, if I didn't fight back so
much, then it wouldn't be such a big deal. But of course now,
because I didn't fight back so much, I'm mad at myself. So I'm
blaming myself. Yeah, that was a really big factor. The first
one—I didn't want to scream or something and have his brother
hear and find out. I just didn't want anyone to know. And the
second time I was thinking, "Well, I'm going to have to see this
person and I don't want it to be a rape. I want it to just stop."
(Laughs.) It didn't. Part of the thinking was that I finally gave
up and just pretended I wasn't there because I thought, "Well,
it won't be a rape." I consciously thought, "Well, I don't want
to be raped, so I'll just let it go."

T: Disappear?

C: Yeah.

T: Didn't work, did it?

C: No. (Laughs.) And that is a big thing I've struggled with because
I've known that I gave up. And so I'm kind of like, "Well, I gave
up because I thought it wouldn't be a rape. . . . "

T: Well, but in a sense—that's not a fair thing to say to yourself. I
think you coped as best you could at the time—

C: Yeah.

T: —with the tools that you had.

C: I know. Right now I'm feeling more that way. I know these
things and I just have to really feel them.* It was weird that I
was shook up for most of last night because of a stupid phone
call. Another big thing is that because I got the thing in the mail
and I called, it's like it's my fault. I'm the one who called him.
I didn't have to call him in the first place. It's like when I went
back to [her attacker's] apartment. I didn't have to go back in
the first place. . . .

T: Well, this is a good one to spend some time on. It's a good little
parallel that happened in the here and now that you can analyze and say, "Let's not take this and run with it the wrong way."

C: Mmm. Yeah.

---

*The client is engaging in emotional reasoning and is confusing thoughts with feelings.
She seems to be saying that once there is affect attached to her thoughts, she really
believes them. Actually, she probably has two competing beliefs, the old one having
affect with it and the newer thought having little emotion. The therapist did not intervene here because she did not want to disrupt the topic being discussed at the time.

T: So what do you want to say to yourself?

C: Um. I don't know. I guess it's okay to say "no." It's okay to hang up. It's okay to be rude.

T: It was also okay to call him up to begin with to get the information.

C: Yeah. It's curiosity.

T: Sure. You have the right to make that phone call. That doesn't mean you've committed to anything.

C: That's true.

The remainder of the session should focus on the theme of esteem. The therapist briefly goes over the module on self-esteem with the client and describes how self-esteem and esteem toward others can be disrupted by rape. The client's self-esteem prior to the rape should be explored. During the session, give the client the Identifying Assumptions sheet (Beck & Emery, 1985) to complete (see handout at the end of the chapter). The client is asked to put a check by each statement that she believes to be true for herself. The therapist should examine whether the checked items are scattered across the three areas (acceptance, competence, control) or whether they primarily fall within one or more areas. If the items fall within one or two the areas, then those specific themes will need particular attention. If the checked items are scattered throughout the sheet, it may indicate that the client has problems with faulty thinking patterns in general (that is, all-or-none thinking).

The therapist will need to explain why these common assumptions are faulty and extreme and how they can lead to depression, anxiety, and poor self-esteem. The client and therapist should also explore the effects of the rape on the development or reinforcement of these assumptions. For homework, the client completes worksheets on stuck points regarding self-esteem using the esteem module and particularly difficult assumptions. In addition to the usual worksheet assignment, ask the client to practice giving and receiving compliments during the week and to do at least one nice thing for herself each day without any conditions or strings attached (for example, take a bubble bath, read a magazine, call a friend to chat). These assignments are given to help the client become comfortable with the idea that she is worthy of compliments and pleasant events without having to earn them or disown them.

Homework Assignment 10

Use the worksheets to confront stuck points regarding self- and other-esteem. Make sure you examine the items you checked on the Identifying Assumptions list in order to identify stuck points regarding esteem, competence, and control. Complete worksheets on some of the most troublesome beliefs.

In addition to the worksheets, practice giving and receiving compliments during the week and do at least one nice thing for yourself each day (without having to earn it). Write down on this sheet what you did for yourself and your reactions to these exercises.

Identifying Assumptions

Acceptance

1. I have to be cared for by someone who loves me.
2. I need to be understood.
3. I can't be left alone.
4. I'm nothing unless I'm loved.
5. To be rejected is the worst thing in the world.
6. I can't get others angry at me.
7. I have to please others.
8. I can't stand being separated from others.
9. Criticism means personal rejection.
10. I can't be alone.

Competence

1. I am what I accomplish.
2. I have to be somebody.
3. Success is everything.
4. There are winners and losers in life.
5. If I'm not on top, I'm a flop.
6. If I let up, I'll fail.
7. I have to be the best at whatever I do.
8. Others' successes take away from mine.
9. If I make a mistake, I'll fail.
10. Failure is the end of the world.

Control

1. I have to be my own boss.
2. I'm the only one who can solve my problems.
3. I can't tolerate others telling me what to do.
4. I can't ask for help.
5. Others are always trying to control me.
6. I have to be perfect to have control.
7. I'm either completely in control or completely out of control.
8. I can't tolerate being out of control.
9. Rules and regulations imprison me.
10. If I let someone get too close, that person will control me.

Module 4: Esteem Issues

I. Beliefs Related to Self—Self-esteem is the belief in your own worth, which is a basic human need. Being understood, respected, and taken seriously is basic to the development of self-esteem.

A. Prior Experience
1. Negative—If you had prior experiences that represented a violation of your sense of self, you are likely to develop negative beliefs about your self-worth. The rape will seem to confirm these beliefs. Prior life experiences that are associated with negative beliefs about the self are likely to be caused by:
   a. Believing other people's negative attitude about you.
   b. An absence of empathy and responsiveness by others.
   c. The experience of being devalued, criticized, or blamed by others.
   d. The belief that you have violated your own ideals or values.
2. Positive—If you had prior experiences that served to enhance your beliefs about your self-worth, then the rape may disrupt those beliefs (your self-esteem). This may be the case if you believed that if a woman is raped there must have been something wrong with her to begin with.

B. Examples of negative beliefs about self-worth include the following:

1. I am bad, destructive, or evil.
2. I am responsible for bad, destructive, or evil acts.
3. I am basically damaged or flawed.
4. I am worthless and deserving of unhappiness and suffering.

C. Symptoms related to negative beliefs include the following:
1. Depression
2. Guilt
3. Shame
4. Possible self-destructive behavior

D. Resolution
1. If you had prior experiences that left you believing that you were worthless (or any of the beliefs listed above in B), the rape will seem to confirm this belief, especially if the rapist said such things to you during the rape or if you received poor social support after the event. In order to improve your self-esteem and reduce the symptoms that often go along with it, you will need to reevaluate your beliefs about your self-worth, and begin to replace maladaptive beliefs with more realistic, positive ones. Possible self-statements include:
   a. Even though something bad happened to me, it does not mean that I am a bad person.
   b. Sometimes bad things happen to good people.
   c. Just because someone says something bad about me does not make it true.
   d. No one deserves to be raped, and that includes me.
   e. Even if I have made mistakes in the past, that does not make me a bad person, deserving of unhappiness or suffering (including the rape).
2. If you had positive beliefs about your self-worth before the rape, you may have believed that "Nothing bad will happen to me because I am a good person." The rape will disrupt such beliefs, and you may begin to think you are a bad person because you were raped, or you may look for reasons why the rape happened to you and what you did to deserve it (for example, "Maybe I was being punished for something I had done or because I am a bad person").

In order to regain your prior positive beliefs about your self-worth, you will need to make some adjustments so that your sense of worth is not disrupted every time something unexpected and bad happens to you. When you can accept that bad things might happen to you (as they happen to everybody from time to time), you let go of blaming yourself for events that you did not cause. Remind yourself that rape is a criminal act of violence, and that no matter what you did (or who you were, what you wore, and so on), it was not your fault. Possible self-statements include:

a. Sometimes bad things happen to good people.
b. If something bad happens to me, it is not necessarily because I did something to cause it or because I deserved it.
c. Sometimes there is no good explanation for why bad things happen.

II. Beliefs Related to Others—These are beliefs about other people that match accurately the reality of the other person and which are reshaped as new information is received. A realistic view of other people is important to psychological health. In less psychologically healthy people, these images are stereotyped, rigid, and relatively unchanged by new information.

A. Prior Experience
1. Negative—If you have had many bad experiences with people in the past or previously had difficulty taking in new information about people you knew (particularly negative information), you may have found yourself surprised, hurt, and betrayed by their actions. You may have concluded that other people are not good or not to be respected. You may have generalized this belief to everyone (even those who are basically good and to be respected). Rape will seem to confirm these beliefs about people.
2. Positive—If your prior experiences with people had been positive and if negative events in the world did not seem to apply to your life, the rape was probably a belief-shattering event. Prior beliefs in the basic goodness of other people may be particularly disrupted if you were raped by an acquaintance or if people whom you assumed would be supportive were not there for you after the rape.

B. Examples of negative other-esteem beliefs include the following:
1. The belief that people are basically uncaring, indifferent, and only out for themselves.
2. The belief that people are bad, evil, or malicious.
3. The belief that the entire human race is bad, evil, or malicious.

C. Symptoms Resulting from Negative Beliefs
1. Chronic anger
2. Contempt
3. Bitterness
4. Cynicism
5. Disbelief when treated with genuine caring compassion ("What do they really want?")
6. Isolation or withdrawal from others
7. Antisocial behavior justified by the belief that people are only out for themselves

D. Resolution
1. It will be important for you to reconsider the automatic assumption that people are no good and to consider how that belief has affected your behavior and social life in general.
   a. When you first meet someone, it is important that you do not form snap judgments, because these tend to be based on stereotypes, which are not generally true for the majority of people you will meet. It is okay to adopt a wait-and-see attitude, which allows you flexibility in developing your perceptions about the other person and does not penalize the person whom you are trying to get to know.
   b. If, over time, this person makes you uncomfortable or does things of which you don't approve, you are free to stop trying to develop the relationship and end it.
   c. Be aware, however, that all people make mistakes, and consider your ground rules for friendships or intimate relationships. If you confront the person with something that makes you uncomfortable, you can use that person's reaction to your request in making a decision about what you want from that person in the future. (For example, if the person is apologetic and makes a genuine effort to avoid

making the same mistake, then you might want to continue getting to know this person. If the person is insensitive to your request or belittles you in some other way,
then you may want to get out of this relationship.)

d. The important point is that, like trust, you need time to
get to know someone and form a valid opinion of her or
him. It is important that you adopt a view of others that is
balanced and allows for changes.

e. A possible self-statement is, "Although there are people I
do not respect and do not wish to know, I cannot assume
this about everyone I meet. I may come to this conclusion
later, but it will be after I have learned more about this
person."

2. If you had prior beliefs that you were a good judge of character,
then being raped by an acquaintance or being betrayed by
those expected to provide social support may shatter this
belief.

a. In the case of the rapist, no one can predict who will rape.
These men tend to be expert manipulators, often fooling
women into believing that they are good and trustworthy.
However, not every man is a manipulator.

b. A possible self-statement is, "I used my best judgment,
and I thought this man was okay. I was fooled, however,
as any person may have been. I can still use caution in
getting to know people but without necessarily assuming
the worst."

c. If those you expected support from let you down, do not
drop these people altogether at first. Talk to them about
how you feel and what you want from them. Use their
reactions to your request as a way of evaluating where you
want the relationship to go.

d. A possible self-statement is, "People sometimes make
mistakes. I will try to find out whether they understand it
was a mistake or whether it reflects a negative character-
istic of that person, which may end the relationship for me
if it is something I cannot accept."

14

Session 11: Esteem Issues

The therapist should reinforce the client's efforts to give and receive compliments and to do nice things for herself (such as taking a long bubble bath, taking time out to read a book or magazine, taking a walk, or buying herself something small). The client is asked how she felt when doing nice things for herself: Did she feel that she did not deserve it? Did she feel guilty? She should be encouraged to continue to do nice things for herself and practice giving and receiving compliments on a daily basis and to allow herself to enjoy them. The therapist can help the client generate some self-statements that enhance self-esteem if she tends to make disparaging comments about herself.

The client and therapist then discuss the worksheets regarding common assumptions and esteem. The stuck points that one client brought to therapy serve as an example within the theme of self-esteem. She described how she realized she partly blamed her mother for the rape and was quite angry at her mother's response afterward. Her mother kicked her out of the house when she was 17 for a few days. It was during that time that she was raped by a "boyfriend" who called her all sorts of names. When she came home and told her mother about the incident, "She called me at least as many names as that guy had called me in the woods. Ugh! She told my dad to burn the clothes I was wearing and fixed me a bubble bath. It was all stupid and degrading. So my stuck point is that I've been angry with my mom for 23 years and I have felt like I was all those names I was called."

Once she was able to acknowledge and feel her anger at her mother and the therapist validated those feelings, the client was able to look more objectively at the accuracy of the names she was called. She was able to "consider the source" of the negative labels and to confront them. She stated that she was not a slut or a whore and that she had many reasons to be proud of herself and her accomplishments. She realized that she had not felt good about herself for a long time and that she had looked to others for the approval that she was unable to give herself. Initially she had difficulty doing nice things for herself (she felt she did not deserve them) and had typically done things for other people. However, once she "gave herself permission," she found herself enjoying it and felt better about herself.

Another example of a self-esteem issue worked on in the homework is depicted on the Challenging Beliefs worksheet on page 122-123. A very common stuck point on the topic of self-esteem is that the client is now damaged in some way because of the rape. This client's automatic belief was that there must have been something wrong with her to begin with for the rapist to have targeted her for assault. By this point in therapy, she was able to challenge this belief herself with the use of the worksheet. However, the therapist was concerned by the statement in Column F (Decatastrophizing) that people could continue to think they can hurt her only if "I let them." The therapist discussed this with the client, and she acknowledged that she could not control what other people thought or did. However, it was also pointed out that she did not need to continue relationships with people who were not responsive to her.

With regard to esteem for others, it is not uncommon for clients to overgeneralize their disregard for the rapist to an entire group. For example, one client decided that all people with money, power, and popularity were bad because the rapist had all of these things.

Challenging Beliefs Worksheet

Column A	Column B	Column C
Situation	**Automatic Thoughts**	**Challenging Your Automatic Thoughts**
Describe the event(s), thought(s), or belief(s) leading to the unpleasant emotion(s).	Write automatic thought(s) preceding emotion(s) in Column A. Rate belief in each automatic thought(s) below from 0-100%.	Use the **Challenging Questions** sheet to examine your automatic thought(s) from Column B.
I perceive myself to be damaged in some way.	*Something must be wrong with me that he thought he could rape me in the first place.* *60%*	*Little factual evidence except the way I feel about myself, "allowing" myself to be betrayed and tricked into thinking he would not hurt me.* *Confusing a habit of thinking about myself as being damaged because of what others have done throughout my lifetime. Reality states it had nothing to do with anything about me that I was raped.*
Emotion(s)		*Judgment of being damaged is based on feelings, therefore, the source is unreliable.*
Specify sad, angry, etc., and rate the degree you feel each emotion from 0-100%. *Sad - 75%* *Frightened - 50%*		

Adapted from Beck & Emery, 1985.

Column D	Column E	Column F
Faulty Thinking Patterns	**Alternative Thoughts**	**Decatastrophizing**
Use the **Faulty Thinking Patterns** sheet to examine your automatic thought(s) from Column B.	What else can I say instead of Column B? How else can I interpret the event instead of Column B? Rate belief in alternative thought(s) from 0-100%.	What's the worst that could ever realistically happen? *People will continue to think they can hurt me throughout my life.*
Drawing conclusion - Men rape for reasons to do with themselves, not with women. *Exaggerating an event - It means that he was violent, not that there's something wrong with me.*	*I was not raped because there was something wrong with me, but because there was something wrong with him.* *75%*	Even if that happened, what could I do? *They can only do that if I let them.*
		Outcome
		Rerate belief in automatic thought(s) in Column B from 0-100%. *30%*
		Specify and rate subsequent emotion(s) from 0-100%. *Sad - 25%* *Frightened - 25%*

She avoided any activities that might lead her to any of these "evils," so much so that she dropped out of school, isolated herself, and took only menial jobs. Another client believed that all attorneys were bad following two trials, the first of which ended in a mistrial (due to the misconduct of the defense attorney). The second trial was more traumatic and devastating to her than the rape in many ways, because she spent 5 days testifying and being criticized for every microdecision or observation she made before, during, and after the assault. The second trial ended in an acquittal. One client stopped dating black men after being raped. After a second rape by a white man, she stopped dating altogether. Exacerbated racism is common after interracial rape. And, of course, many rape victims generalize their beliefs about the rapist to the entire male gender.

Selective attention is another way in which beliefs about the "goodness-badness" of humans are affected following rape. Before being assaulted, many women pay little attention to reports about crime in the media. After being raped, they begin to notice how often the topic emerges in newspapers, on television news and programs, and in magazines. Because they are now attending to crime, it appears to them that crime is everywhere and that all people are bad. They forget that these events are being reported because they are "news," and that most people are neither victimizing nor being victimized on a daily basis.

In these cases in which all of humanity or some subgroup of the population is maligned by the victim, it is important for the therapist to help her move from the extreme and down the continuum. The client will need to look for and acknowledge the exceptions to her overgeneralized schema in order to accommodate the schema more realistically.

The topic of intimacy is introduced toward the end of the session, and the therapist and client briefly discuss how it may have been affected by the rape. Intimacy with others (or lack of intimacy) will be easier to identify than self-intimacy. Self-intimacy is the ability to soothe and calm oneself and to be alone without feeling lonely or empty. The client is encouraged to recognize how intimacy with herself and others was before the rape and how it was affected by the assault. The therapist and client should discuss any problems with inappropriate external attempts to self-soothe (for example, alcohol, food, and spending). Again, the client should use the worksheets and list of questions for homework to confront maladaptive self-statements and to generate more comforting statements.

Finally, in order to assess how the client's beliefs have changed since the start of treatment, the client is asked to rewrite the first assignment on what it now means to her that she was raped.

Homework Assignment 11

Use the worksheets to confront stuck points regarding self- and other-intimacy. Continue completing worksheets on previous topics that are still problematic.

Also please write at least one page on what it means to you that you were raped. Please consider the effects that rape now has on your beliefs about yourself, others, and the world. Also consider the following topics while writing your answer: safety, trust, power and control, esteem, and intimacy.

Continue to do nice things for yourself on a daily basis. Also continue to practice giving and receiving compliments.

Module 5: Intimacy Issues

I. Beliefs Related to Self—An important function for stability is the ability to soothe and calm oneself. This self-intimacy is reflected in the ability to be alone without feeling lonely or empty. When a trauma occurs, people react differently depending on their expectancy regarding how well they will cope.

A. Prior Experience
1. Negative—If you had prior experiences (or poor role models) that led you to believe that you are unable to cope with negative life events, you may have reacted to the rape with negative beliefs that you were unable to soothe, comfort, or nurture yourself.
2. Positive—A person with stable and positive self-intimacy may experience the rape as less traumatic because of her expectancy of drawing support from internal resources.

3. However, if the event is so severe that a person is unable to soothe herself, then the event is in conflict with earlier self-intimacy beliefs. The person may feel overwhelmed or flooded by anxiety.

B. Symptoms of Negative Beliefs
1. Inability to comfort and soothe self
2. Fear of being alone
3. Experience of inner emptiness or deadness
4. Periods of great anxiety or panic if reminded of trauma when alone
5. May look to external sources of comfort: food, drugs, alcohol, medications, spending money, or sex
6. Needy or demanding relationships

C. Resolution
1. Understanding the normal reactions following rape may help you feel less panicky about what you are experiencing. Realizing that most people cannot recover from such a major traumatic event without the support of others is also important. Finally, it is important to recognize that external sources of comfort such as alcohol or food are simply crutches that, instead of helping you recover, may prolong your reactions. They may comfort you in the short run because you use them to avoid and suppress your feelings. The feelings do not go away, however, and you then also have to deal with the consequences of the excess food, spending, alcohol, and so on, which just compounds the problem.
2. Possible self-statements include:
   I will recover from this rape.
   I will not suffer forever.
   I can soothe myself and use the skills I have learned to cope with these negative feelings.
   I may need help in dealing with my reactions, but that is normal.
   Even though my feelings are quite strong and unpleasant to experience, I know they are temporary and will fade over time.
   The skills and abilities I am developing now will help me to cope better with other stressful situations in the future.

II. Beliefs Related to Others—The longing for intimacy, connection, and closeness is one of the most basic human needs. The capacity to be intimately connected with other people is fragile. It can easily be damaged or destroyed through insensitive, hurtful, or nonempathetic responses from others.

A. Prior Experience
1. Negative—Negative beliefs may result from traumatic loss of intimate connections. The rape may confirm your belief in your inability to be close to another person.
2. Positive—If you previously had satisfying intimate relationships with others, you may find that the rape (especially if committed by an acquaintance) may leave you believing that you could never be intimate with anyone again.

B. Post-Rape Experience—You may also experience a disruption in your belief about your ability to be intimate with others if you were blamed or rejected by those you thought would be supportive.

C. Symptoms Resulting from Negative Beliefs
1. Pervasive loneliness
2. Emptiness or isolation
3. Person may fail to experience connectedness with others even in relationships that are genuinely loving and intimate.

D. Resolution
1. In order for you to again have intimate relationships with others, you will need to adopt new, more adaptive beliefs about intimacy. Intimate relationships take time to develop and involve effort from both people. You are not solely responsible for the failure of prior relationships. The development of relationships involves risk taking, and it is possible that you may be hurt again. Staying away from relationships for this reason alone, however, is likely to leave you feeling empty and alone.
2. Possible self-statements regarding new relationships include: Even though a former relationship did not work out, it does not mean that I cannot have satisfying intimate relationships in the future.

I cannot continue to believe and behave as though everyone will betray me.

I will need to take risks in developing relationships in the future, but if I take it slow, I will have a better chance of telling whether this person can be trusted.

I am unlikely to be raped again.

3. Attempt to resolve your issues with the people who let you down and hurt you by asking them for what you need and letting them know how you feel about what they said or did.

4. If they are unable to adjust to your requests and are unable to give you what you need, you may decide that you can no longer be close to those people. You may find, however, that they responded as they did from ignorance or fear. As a result of your efforts, communication may improve and you may end up feeling closer to them than you did before the rape.

5. Possible self-statements about existing relationships include:

I can still be close to people, but I may not be able (or want) to be intimate with everyone I meet.

I may lose prior or future intimate relationships with others who cannot meet me halfway, but this is not my fault or because I did not try.

15

Session 12: Intimacy Issues and Meaning of the Event

The final session begins with a discussion of the homework on intimacy. The purpose of the session is to help the client identify her stuck points regarding intimacy. The goal for the client is to work on these stuck points over time with the new skills she has learned in therapy.

Problems with self-intimacy are evident if the client has been abusing substances, including food. When given the assignment to write about the rape, one client announced that she would have to eat a gallon of ice cream and smoke two packs of cigarettes to get through it. This was a good clue to the therapist that she had issues about self-comforting. Over the course of the therapy and particularly during these last two sessions, this issue was addressed. Several of our other clients had been hospitalized for eating disorders (anorexia and bulimia) prior to receiving treatment with us. It was during treatment for those disorders that they became aware of the connection between the rapes and their eating disorders. These issues about self-soothing are often related to control issues, so the issue of substance abuse is frequently addressed earlier in treatment as well. Rather than grabbing for food, cigarettes, or alcohol, these women were encouraged to grab a worksheet instead and to think through what they were saying to themselves and to calm themselves with more appropriate self-statements and behaviors.

With regard to intimacy with others, two types of intimacy are often issues: (1) closeness with family and friends and (2) sexual intimacy. Many women who have been raped withdraw from people who could be supportive and they avoid being close to others as a way of protecting themselves from possible rejection or blame. Frequently, relationships dissolve, and the women avoid dating or developing new relationships. As a result, many of these women feel isolated and alone during their recovery from the rape. Sexual intimacy becomes particularly threatening because the act of being sexual has become a cue associated with the rape and because of the level of trust and vulnerability that is necessary for intimacy. Their withdrawal, however, is in direct conflict with their need for comfort and support from others. These intimacy issues are often interwoven with trust issues that may still be unresolved and which deserve continued attention from the client.

One woman who had been raped by a stranger had concluded that no man could be trusted. Even though she had a close relationship with a boyfriend prior to the rape, she found herself withdrawing from him and getting angry at him after the rape. She also avoided sexual contact with him not because of his behavior (he was quite patient and not insistent at all), but because sexual contact reminded her of the rape and she tended to have fear reactions and flashbacks when they became physically intimate. The therapist helped the client to see that her boyfriend was actually very gentle and did not act at all as the rapist had. By looking at his behavior more objectively (with a worksheet and the therapist), the client realized that she had every reason to believe that he was trustworthy. The therapist advised the client not to avoid sex but to take control and initiate contact. She was advised that if she became frightened or had a flashback, they were to stop for a few minutes and to just hold each other until she calmed down again. She could then proceed; she was encouraged not to quit. At the next session (this session), she reported that this technique had been successful and that she was feeling more comfortable and in control.

The Challenging Beliefs worksheet that follows on page 132-133 contains an example of a stuck point on intimacy. This worksheet was written by the same woman who wrote the example in Chapter 14 on self-esteem. This same stuck point affected different areas of functioning. Besides believing that she must have been raped because there was something wrong with her to begin with, she also believed that men would believe she was damaged or incapable of having a healthy relationship because of the rape or would be turned off because of her assault. She had generalized these beliefs from a single experience, but in working with the sheet she quickly realized she was overgeneralizing and was able to generate another way to view the situation. This client had withdrawn socially, but at one of the follow-up assessment sessions, she stated that she had started dating again.

The therapist and client should go over the new essay regarding the meaning of the rape. The client should be encouraged to examine how her beliefs have changed as a result of the work she has done in therapy. The therapist should also look for any remaining distortions or faulty beliefs that may need further intervention. Many clients notice a change in what they had originally written, mostly in terms of increased self-understanding and a growing belief that they somehow gained something positive from the rape (that is, from the therapy that followed the rape). The following are examples of the first and last essay written by a woman who had been raped by an acquaintance many years ago. It clearly illustrates the issue with which she struggled throughout therapy—self-blame—and the progress she made.

CASE EXAMPLE 10 (HOMEWORK 1)

What it has meant to me to be raped has been a big question to me for a long time. Being raped meant taking something from me I wasn't freely giving. It meant taking advantage of me when my guard was down. I've always been shy, never speaking up, always trying to please other people more than myself. The rape caused me to close even more

Challenging Beliefs Worksheet

Column A	Column B	Column C
Situation	**Automatic Thoughts**	**Challenging Your Automatic Thoughts**
Describe the event(s), thought(s), or belief(s) leading to the unpleasant emotion(s).	Write automatic thought(s) preceding emotion(s) in Column A. Rate belief in each automatic thought(s) below from 0-100%.	Use the **Challenging Questions** sheet to examine your automatic thought(s) from Column B.
I am damaged because I was raped.	*Men won't want to have relationships with me if they know I've been raped because they will think I'm damaged or incapable of having healthy relationships.* *75%*	*I told a man about the rape while we were dating and he said it would not bother him, but then acted like it did, and stopped sexual relations for some time. Since I don't tell most people about it, I don't know if they would all feel that way.* *All or none and exaggerated thinking - Most healthy men would not run from a relationship.* *Information is unreliable because it comes from past negative experience and an unhealthy man.* *Thinking in terms of certainties and high probabilities.*
Emotion(s)		
Specify sad, angry, etc., and rate the degree you feel each emotion from 0-100%. *Fear - 50%* *Sadness - 80%* *Anger - 50%*		

Adapted from Beck & Emery, 1985.

Column D	Column E	Column F
Faulty Thinking Patterns	**Alternative Thoughts**	**Decatastrophizing**
Use the **Faulty Thinking Patterns** sheet to examine your automatic thought(s) from Column B.	What else can I say instead of Column B? How else can I interpret the event instead of Column B? Rate belief in alternative thought(s) from 0-100%.	What's the worst that could ever <u>realistically</u> happen? *A man would tell me he didn't want anything to do with me because of the rape.*
Exaggerated event - Because one man may have had problems dealing with it does not mean others will. *Oversimplifying - If I tell someone who can't deal with that, it's not necessarily bad because I could find out something important about the relationship.*	*If I tell a man about the rape, he won't necessarily think I'm flawed or damaged. Not everyone will understand, but if I choose men who are healthy and use good judgment about who I tell, I can find a man who is sensitive.*	Even if that happened, what could I do? *Find someone who is healthy and secure.*
Overgeneralizing from one man - Just because he couldn't deal with it does not mean that I'm damaged. It means he's not capable.		Outcome
		Rerate belief in automatic thought(s) in Column B from 0-100%. *50%*
Disregarding important aspects of a situation - He was not healthy or secure.		
		Specify and rate subsequent emotion(s) from 0-100%. *Fear - 25%* *Sadness - 40%* *Anger - 10%*

to other people (at times). I have a very difficult time trusting men especially when left alone with them. I'm scared, always thinking in the back of my mind how I would defend myself if that man were to attack me. It bothers me that I have to feel that way and not trust many people. Before the rape when I was left alone with a man, my thoughts always drifted to . . . was he interested in me, did he find me attractive. After the rape, I would get the shakes being left alone with a man. My husband thought when we first started going out that he was my first date ever. But after we got to know one another I think I latched onto him, not only because I loved him, but because I felt secure with him. When he asked me to marry him, I was excited because I wouldn't have to date anymore. Since my rape was kind of a date rape, I didn't want to deal with dating anymore. (Don't misunderstand—I made sure I loved him before I married him.) The rape didn't affect my intimacy because I totally dissociated the rape from the relationship and intimacy of my husband. The rape was scary. I was hurt during the rape— there was no love or kindness at all. My husband is always kind, gentle. I think that's one reason why the rape never affected my intimacy.

I had always been nervous and sort of scared to be alone. But now being alone and nervous and scared, those feelings have the rape tacked onto them. For instance, if we were to be robbed, I would most likely be raped. When shopping, I always check the inside of my car before getting in. When my husband travels, the garage and basement have to be checked before I can sleep somewhat comfortably.

I think that as far as the world is concerned there are a lot of good people and there are a lot of evil people and the scary thing is that you can't tell them apart. That disturbs me.

As far as others are concerned, it takes me a lot longer to befriend people and take them into my little shell and trust them.

As far as myself, my self-esteem has never been very good and always tied to what others thought of me. This man shattered any self-esteem or respect I had for myself. And I have a very difficult time trusting my judgments and decisions. I always have to have second opinions. That makes me angry.

CASE EXAMPLE 10 (HOMEWORK 11)

What it means to me that I was raped is that an acquaintance intimidated me and took that which was not freely given. Not only did he take sex but he took my trust in myself, he took my feeling of control, and he shattered my self-esteem. I will always hate him for that. But one thing I won't allow him to take is my determination to get them back. It's time for me to grab the bull by the horns and lead it where I want it to go. I foresee a long road but I'm anxious to travel down it.

I believed for a long time that the rape was my fault. I don't believe that anymore and that is a great relief. I know I was frightened and I did what I felt I had to do to survive. I wouldn't freely do those things normally. There wasn't any tenderness—it was all violently taken. Coming to that realization has brought about a lot of peace of mind and also the avenue for healing. I'll never be the person I was before and part of me is sad for that, but part of me knows, in time, I'll be stronger because of the rape . . . in time.

The rest of the session is saved for review of all the concepts and skills that have been introduced over the course of therapy. The client is reminded that her success in recovering will depend on her persistence in continuing to practice her new skills and resistance to returning to old avoidance patterns or faulty thinking patterns. Any remaining stuck points should be identified and strategies for confronting should be reiterated. Clients are asked to reflect on the progress and changes they have made during the course of therapy and are encouraged to take credit for facing and dealing with a very difficult and traumatic event. Goals for the future are discussed. Clients who also have a history of incest are encouraged to seek out further treatment in order to deal more directly with those issues.

PART III

SPECIAL CONSIDERATIONS

16

Group Versus Individual Treatment

CPT has been implemented in both individual and group formats. Although comparative analyses have not yet been conducted, both formats appear to be equally effective as based on the SCID interviews pre- and posttreatment. For the most part, we have allowed the women to choose which format they prefer depending on the availability of a group and therapists. Because we are known to have both formats available, prospective clients who contact us usually express a clear preference.

There are advantages and disadvantages to both formats. One advantage of the group format is probably the facilitation of cognitive and emotional processing by means of the other group members. Seeing other women who have been raped demonstrates very quickly the reality that rape victims look and act very normal. There is nothing about women who have been raped, either in their appearance or behavior, that marks them as having experienced rape. For those clients who tend to perceive others as not understanding how they feel, feedback from group members, whom they know have been raped, may carry more credibility than would feedback from a therapist.

139

Frequently, clients with PTSD symptoms fear that they are crazy and are experiencing uniquely bad reactions. Meeting other rape victims and hearing about their reactions quickly normalizes their experience and reduces their sense of isolation. Another advantage of group format is the subtle social pressure for the group members to complete their homework. When a client fails to do her homework and sees the other group members complete theirs with some benefit, she is more quickly convinced of the effectiveness of working outside the sessions.

Finally, a group format provides the clients with a social support network that they may not have outside of therapy. Typically, the advice they have received from family and friends is to forget about the rape, put it behind them, and not think about it (they facilitate avoidance symptoms). These people may not understand why the client continues to have reactions and may not be supportive of a therapy that asks the client to do the opposite of what they have advised.

Some of the disadvantages of a group format include the pragmatic difficulty of recruiting enough clients at any given time to start a group, and less individual attention for each group member. If one group member is much more dominant than the others, if one client has a severe personality disorder, or if a traumatic event occurs to one member during the course of the group, it may be difficult to stay on track.

An obvious advantage of individual therapy is that the therapist can give exclusive attention to one client and her issues. There is more time for in-session flooding, and the therapist can more thoroughly challenge underlying cognitions. In addition, some clients are not comfortable in a group setting and are more likely to fully disclose their experiences, beliefs, and reactions in a more private setting.

❏ Differences Between Group and Individual CPT

CPT is very similar whether conducted with a group of women or with a single client. The greatest difference is in the implementation of the exposure component. While women in individual therapy are given an additional opportunity to reexperience their emotions in a one-on-one setting during sessions (in addition to experiencing the same between sessions), we do not allow group members to read their accounts out loud during therapy sessions. While processing one's own rape is important, hearing the graphic details of another woman's rape is likely to produce secondary traumatization in someone already suffering from PTSD.

Instead, during the session, the therapists explore the reactions the clients had while writing about the rape to determine whether they in fact experienced prolonged exposure. Clients are asked whether they included sensory details, thoughts, and feelings in their account; experienced strong emotions; or recalled new memories. If group members were unable to express their emotions fully, they are encouraged to take steps to increase the likelihood of successfully completing the assignment.

Following this discussion, the therapists collect the written accounts to read between sessions. While reading the accounts, the therapists search for stuck points, which are usually indicated by points at which the client stopped writing and drew a line, or parts of the event she skips, glosses over, or reports amnesia for. The therapist makes note of whether the account has been written like a police report (without accompanying thoughts and feelings) or whether the full schema has been retrieved. Encouragement, praise, and possible stuck points are recorded on the accounts before they are returned.

The groups we have conducted have been closed; that is, once a group has started, no new members may join. The closed format is, of course, necessary because CPT was developed as a progressive therapy in which skills are taught in a particular order and build upon one another. While individual therapy sessions typically last 50 to 60 minutes, group sessions run 90 minutes to allow the members adequate time to discuss their particular issues. Ideally, groups should have between four and nine members. We have found that four members is minimal, because if someone misses a session then the group ceases to be a group and becomes individual therapy with several clients in attendance. Nine is the absolute maximum, because if the group becomes too large there is not enough time for the individual members to get their needs met, and the large size inhibits individual disclosures.

Although it is possible for one therapist to run a group, we recommend two cotherapists. While one therapist is presenting new material or facilitating the discussions, the other therapist can observe the reactions of the other group members and bring them into the discussion. Also, pragmatically, it is difficult for one therapist to go over all of the homework and respond to the writing assignments in a thorough manner.

If an individual-therapy client misses a session, it can be rescheduled or delayed until the next scheduled appointment. However, the same opportunity is not possible with groups. Instead, if a client misses a group session, she is contacted by telephone. If the next homework assignment can be given over the phone, the therapist does so and asks the client how the last assignment went. Another purpose for the telephone call is to discuss why the client missed the session and to discuss the problem of avoidance if indicated. If necessary, the therapist invites the client to arrive early for the next session so the last session can be reviewed and the homework given.

Thus far, we have not had a problem with clients missing more than a few sessions. If someone were to miss many sessions and had not been doing the homework, we would discuss the problem with the client to try to determine if she needed individual therapy or whether she was unwilling to change her avoidance patterns at this time. We would encourage her to begin therapy again when she felt ready to confront her issues. We would also offer other referrals.

Although we discourage clients from receiving therapy for the rape from other therapists while in treatment with us, our groups have sometimes been considered adjunctive therapy for women who are already receiving individual therapy elsewhere. Typically, they are working on other issues with their individual therapist and have come to us because their therapist was not dealing with their rape issues. We believe that receiving simultaneous rape-focused therapy with both group and individual therapists can be very confusing for the client, especially if the individual therapist assumes a different theoretical orientation.

17

Practical Considerations for Running Groups

Linda M. Housman

Monica K. Schnicke

❑ Personality Style and Interpersonal Conflict Between Group Members

When running groups, differences in personality styles and inter-personal conflict are inherent to the process. These are normal occur-rences that should be anticipated. Therapists, however, should be prepared to deal with these issues in order to ensure that the group runs smoothly and that members get the most from their experience.

There are a couple of personality styles that we have noted as requiring special attention. People who have a dominant commu-nication style tend to express their thoughts frequently, sometimes to the extent that other group members are slighted. This not only quiets those who want to talk, but also creates even more of a challenge for the shy or quiet client who already has a difficult time expressing herself. Also, given the avoidant nature of rape-treatment groups, the dominant group member will only exacerbate this problem. Those members who are reluctant to talk no longer have to talk: They have sufficient reason not to participate.

In order to ensure that all group members have the opportunity to benefit from the therapeutic effects of disclosure and expression, it is essential that the therapists identify those members who have a tendency to dominate the group. It is also important that the therapists recognize those members who have a difficult time expressing themselves either because of shyness or avoidance. After these client styles have been identified, the therapists need to loosely monitor the amount of time that the members are speaking. It may then be necessary to help the dominant member close down and summarize her thoughts.

In terms of the shy or less expressive client, we have dealt with these individuals in a couple of different ways, depending on the client and the personal style of the therapist. One approach is to gently address them within the context of the group. Statements such as, "Mary, we've not heard from you yet this evening—I wonder if you have anything that you would like to share with us before we leave this topic?" might elicit a response. If the client does not respond to this approach after a couple of attempts, it is often more helpful to approach her outside of the group setting. This enables the therapists to assess any problems or difficulties that the client may be having that prevent her from talking in group.

On occasion, you will find that certain members of the group do not get along. In essence, one or more group members may be ostracized simply because other group members do not like them. When this happens, the excluded member(s) may not be given the opportunity to talk or may be cut off prematurely when they are speaking to the group. Because communication and support are crucial aspects of a successful therapy group, and even more so for rape victims, estranged members probably will not find the group helpful and may even feel harmed.

The therapists must provide more direct intervention in these cases to ensure that all group members are feeling supported and connected to the group. This requires that therapists attend to group dynamics and monitor those members who may not be fully participating due to the lack of support from the group. For example, if it is noted that a member of the group is feeling alienated or shunned, it is the responsibility of the therapist to bring the person back into the group by directing comments toward them or in some other way engaging the member in order to decrease feelings of isolation.

Sometimes the therapists may notice tension between members immediately after group has started. When this has been the case in the past, we have found that it is most appropriate to make a process intervention before problems get out of hand. Specifically, we have told group members close to the start of the group that we like to check in periodically with them in order to assess how comfortable they are feeling and how much support they feel they are getting. We also stress that we are interested in hearing their suggestions about what might be done differently in order to make members feel safe and supported. The therapists should follow through on this without haste (that is, the next session), leaving some time after the inquiry to process the responses and suggestions of group members. Checking in again after a few sessions is helpful for getting feedback on adjustments made, if any.

❑ Not Completing Homework

Incomplete homework is one of the most common problems encountered in running CPT groups. Although there is added pressure to complete homework assignments because group members, as well as therapists, will know if the homework is not completed, some clients will still have difficulty completing assignments. There are a couple of reasons why clients are reluctant to complete assignments, both of which involve avoidance of some kind.

We have found, for the most part, that homework noncompletion reflects avoidance of material that is emotionally laden. Given that all CPT participants are diagnosed with PTSD before entering therapy, this is understandable and somewhat expected. It is important that the client herself be able to verbalize her fear of confronting her thoughts, feelings, and memories. Fears are usually focused on the belief that her intense feelings will destroy her or be too overwhelming if experienced fully. This particular belief can be viewed as yet another stuck point that must be challenged in order for the client to utilize and benefit from the CPT model. We have found that it is especially helpful at the beginning of therapy to predict that avoidance of thoughts and feelings, which is likely to be reflected in homework assignments, may be an issue. This also serves the purpose of normalizing the clients' initial resistance to confronting difficult material.

Similarly, some group members have a difficult time completing written homework assignments because the act of writing their experiences on paper makes the event and their reactions too real to deny. This tendency to deny can be very strong in those women who have been unable to label their experiences as rape. Typically, these are the women who come to the group with doubts as to whether what happened to them was actually a rape.

It is important that the therapists do not let these doubts go unchallenged but instead point out that the very fact that they are so traumatized provides evidence that the event was rape. Women who engage in normal sexual activity do not have traumatic reactions such as PTSD. It may also be helpful to ask them why they think they are participating in a rape group—how is it that they are here? This question can help point out the discrepancy between what turns out to be two sets of thoughts about the assault. By labeling the experience as a rape, the client is then able to make sense out of the overwhelming emotions she is experiencing and is better able to explore the impact that the event has had on her life. This is the first step toward recovery.

❏ Members Getting Too Emotional

The CPT model has been presented at various seminars and conventions. One question that has often been asked is what to do when clients become too emotional. The answer to this question may seem simple at first, but it is nonetheless true. We believe that there is no such thing as clients becoming too emotional. The question may, in fact, reflect the therapist's discomfort with emotions.

One of the goals of therapy with trauma victims in general is to create an atmosphere that is safe enough for them to experience their full range of emotions. Rape victims often report that external sources of support do not allow them to feel their feelings about their experience. Many people, especially those closest to the victim, are at a loss as to how to be supportive. As such, they believe the best way to help is to encourage the victim to put the event "behind her" or "pretend it didn't happen and get on with your life." Unfortunately, the victim cannot do this and recover at the same time. The event has not been fully processed.

Another common fear that a rape victim may have, which is confirmed by those who encourage her to put the event away, is that her emotions are too much for either herself or others to handle. By the time the client enters the group, she is often convinced that she has no safe place or outlet for her emotions—that they are, in fact, too dangerous. She may also be convinced that if she does let her feelings surface, they will destroy her and those around her.

It is the therapist's responsibility to guide the client through her feelings and show her that they are manageable and acceptable. The best way to do this is to elicit the feelings through feeling statements, such as "That must have been very frightening for you," or "As you talk about this, I hear a lot of anger. . . . Can you tell me more about how you are feeling right now?" or simply, "You look very sad as you say that." This also implicitly sends a message to the client that her feelings are acceptable to express and that you, the therapist, can handle them. We have found that such encouragement facilitates the expression and subsequent extinction of strong emotional responses by the client and also confirms that her feelings are indeed manageable and appropriate.

One caveat should be added, however. We do not implement this therapy with women with borderline personalities and an inability to regulate affect. If a client has a history of self-mutilation or other parasuicidal behavior, she should not receive any type of exposure-based therapy until she is stable and more able to cope with strong affect. Because we screen out women with severe competing pathology from this brief therapy, we have had no problems with suicidal or parasuicidal behavior.

❑ Staying on Task

One challenge encountered by every therapist, at some time or another, is keeping the client "on task." This challenge is not absent in rape groups. In fact, given the content of the material being discussed and the client's reluctance (that is, avoidance) to immerse herself fully in her thoughts and feelings, therapists can expect group members to hit every point except the pertinent one. This is especially true in the beginning when avoidance tends to be the most severe.

It will be important that the therapists provide some structure by explaining at the start what must be covered in each session. Most groups can stay on task if the therapists set an agenda for the session. This agenda should include discussing the previous week's homework assignment and introducing the next topic and assignment. It is helpful to leave the last 20-30 minutes to introduce the new topic.

Setting the agenda, however, does not necessarily ensure that group members will stay focused on the issue at hand. There will be times when a client will stray far from her original thought. We have found that this often occurs when the subject matter becomes too emotionally laden. This may make the client feel out of control and often triggers avoidant behavior (that is, getting off task). In an attempt to regain control, she may digress to something less threatening.

It is the therapist's responsibility to see that the group uses its time wisely. We predict and normalize the desire to avoid discussing rape-related issues, but we also clarify that recovery depends on the members' ability to confront their issues head on and to work through their stuck points. Breaking the avoidance cycle is one of the most challenging tasks for clients and requires that the therapists be able to recognize and intervene when this happens.

If a group member is veering off topic, it is important that the therapist bring her back to her original thought. Saying something like "I'm not sure I see the connection between what you are saying now and the topic that you originally started with. . . . Can you explain this further?" can be helpful. Gentle confrontation of repeated avoidance is also appropriate. A comment such as "It sounds as though it is very difficult for you to stay with your feelings about this issue" can elicit a "Yes . . . because I am afraid that if I do. . . . " response from the client. This response enables the therapist to help the client challenge the underlying fears or other issues that stimulate her avoidance.

18

Client Characteristics
That May Affect Treatment

Several client characteristics and situational variables should be considered when deciding whether to implement a brief form of therapy such as CPT. Some of these variables will influence the mode of therapy and are considered screening issues. Others will impact on the course of treatment but will not necessarily prevent the implementation of CPT.

❏ Incest History

It is fairly common for women who seek treatment for rape to report a history of incest or give indications that they may have such a history. When asked about inappropriate sexual touch as a child, a woman without such a history is fairly clear that there has been no abuse. A woman with a history of child sexual abuse may be able to answer affirmatively or may express some doubt or confusion about the question. Occasionally, someone with such a history will deny abuse. Do not rule out the possibility, however, if she reports blocks of amnesia for her childhood, presents with a borderline personality, reports having alcoholic or dysfunctional parents, or reports more than two rapes by different people. Although two rapes are fairly common in those who have no incest history (25% of those completing our treatment), it is rare to encounter women who have been raped multiple times without a history of incest (excluding marital rape). These indicators should be considered "red flags" to the therapist that this is someone who may begin to uncover child sexual abuse during therapy. Exposure types of therapy, such as CPT, which elicit strong affect, are likely to begin triggering other traumatic memories.

The decision to begin CPT with clients who have incest histories depends on where they are with their uncovering or recovery from their child sexual abuse. If a client is relatively stable and has dealt with her incest issues in therapy, then CPT is appropriate. Although the focus of CPT is on the rape and not the incest, as the therapist and client begin to work on the five areas of beliefs (safety, trust, power, esteem, and intimacy), the client's history can be examined with regard to how beliefs evolving from the incest affected beliefs about the rape. Both sets of beliefs can be modified in therapy.

If a client is just beginning to uncover the incest and is fluctuating between strong affect and denial, it is probably best to have her begin open-ended therapy rather than to contract for 12 sessions. It is unlikely that she will be able to process the rape thoroughly without the incest intruding. And if she is fragile with regard to coping skills and has suicidal depression or other self-destructive behaviors, it will be necessary to stabilize her before any exposure work should be attempted. An elongated version of CPT is appropriate for the treatment of incest as well as rape, but it should not be attempted before the client's behavior and affect have been regulated.

When incest is suspected but not remembered, the client's fragility should be the guideline as to whether to begin CPT. Given any of the red flags listed above, the therapist may wish to inform the client that because of the amnesia, other prior traumas are suspected and that following CPT, the client may wish to receive additional ongoing therapy to deal with any current life problems beyond the rape and to begin to deal with family issues. The women who arrive for treatment with childhood amnesias, family alcoholism, and so on often have chaotic lives and other current problems in addition to reactions to the rape.

❏ **Substance Abuse**

We do not implement CPT with someone who is currently abusing alcohol or drugs. In fact, CPT is not recommended for someone who has recently achieved sobriety but still feels at risk for relapse. For example, recently we treated two women who had stopped drinking prior to initiating treatment. One had stopped drinking 3 months before starting treatment and had been attending Alcoholics Anonymous 5 days a week. The other had not been drinking for several years and was working in an alcohol-treatment program. The first woman was confident and determined about her decision to quit drinking and did not feel at risk for relapse. She completed CPT very successfully. The other woman completed 12 sessions, but she was extremely avoidant and missed many sessions along the way, refused to do the homework, and when encouraged to remember the rape, responded by saying that she was committed to staying off alcohol, which implied that she was afraid if she felt her emotions about the rape, she would resume drinking.

If it is clear to the therapist that the client is fragile with regard to sobriety, then CPT should not be implemented as it is currently laid out. The exposure component will probably be too stressful or overwhelming. If drinking had been adopted as an avoidance behavior, the strong emotions and memories uncovered during CPT may tempt the client to resume drinking to suppress her memories, cognitions, and feelings.

However, CPT can be implemented with clients who are comfortable with their sobriety and are aware of the necessity to deal directly with strong emotions during therapy. If the urge to drink or use drugs arises in the context of CPT, some of the cognitive techniques could be used to modify maladaptive self-statements associated with drinking as a means of coping. The therapist should pay special attention to other avoidance strategies with this type of client and strongly encourage completion of homework so that new means of coping are learned and then available for use.

It is important to note that it is not uncommon for women to increase their alcohol use following rape. Normally, this does not lead to addiction and is used temporarily as a coping (avoidance) strategy. Excessive food consumption is also very common. External substances serve as self-soothing strategies (see Chapter 15) and as ways of avoiding painful emotions. Weight gain also serves as an interpersonal avoidance strategy. If the client makes herself unattractive, she believes she is less likely to get raped again (or even become intimate with someone). As long as the use of these external substances does not significantly interfere with the client's functioning, CPT can be initiated. These issues, however, may need to be broached earlier in therapy than the last session if it is clear that they are interfering with recovery.

❏ Marital Rape

We have not excluded marital rape victims from group format CPT therapy. Recently, we have seen an increase in the number of marital rape victims seeking treatment. However, there are some special considerations for therapists to consider when working with marital rape victims. First, the client is likely to have been subjected to multiple rapes over an extended period of time. In addition, the sexual abuse is usually committed within the context of extensive physical or emotional abuse. Finally, several of our clients have had children resulting from rape(s) and have strong ambivalent feelings about their children as well as shame and guilt about this ambivalence. They have often arrived in therapy in the midst of messy and complicated divorce and custody battles. Unlike most other rape victims, these women often are forced to face their assailants again and again under circumstances that tend to complicate their reactions to the rape(s) and intensify ambivalent feelings.

A study that compared raped *and* battered women with women who were battered found that raped and battered women report significantly more problems with self-esteem, fear, depression, hostility, and sexual functioning (Shields, Resick, & Hanneke, 1990). Because of the number of rapes and the range of problems experienced, it is likely that marital rape victims will need more extensive treatment than 12 sessions as laid out with CPT. The exposure component (writing and discussing the crimes) will need to be extended to encompass the range of incidents that occurred, particularly those involving bizarre or deviant behavior on the part of the husband/ rapist. The cognitive component will need to address conflicts regarding the tremendous discrepancy between the woman's previously idealistic or naive views of her marriage and the reality of her experience. Such women often also have ambivalent feelings regarding their spouses that need to be addressed and normalized. Other issues that often arise with marital rape victims include blaming themselves for their repeated victimization, seriously doubting their judgment and behavior, criticizing their inability to extricate themselves sooner, believing that their husbands control their lives (even after physical separation), and facing more disbelief from family members and friends who have difficulty comprehending their situation. The therapist should address and normalize all of these issues while at the same time helping the client challenge and replace any maladaptive self-statements.

❏ Personality Disorders

Most of the women we have worked with have had post-traumatic stress disorder and sometimes major depression, without any comorbid personality disorders. However, some clients do have personality disorders that have an impact on the course of treatment. The three personality disorders we encounter most frequently in our work with rape victims are dependent, avoidant, and borderline. All three types may complicate and extend therapy.

When conducting group therapy, we attempt to screen out women with borderline personality by screening out those with incest histories. Most women with borderline personality have histories of childhood sexual abuse. Although group therapy may be beneficial for those with borderline personality disorders, the group should be tailored for that type of disorder. Having one woman with borderline personality in a short-term group with fairly healthy women meets no one's needs. From our experience, the following problems emerge: (1) the borderline client is unable to establish trust quickly enough to benefit from such brief, problem-focused therapy; (2) the exposure component tends to uncover many other traumas that, when combined with the borderline client's propensity for parasuicidal behavior, overwhelm the rest of the group as well as the client; and (3) the tendency of these women to move initially from crisis to crisis distracts other group members from dealing with their own rape-related issues.

We sometimes provide individual CPT for those women who exhibit borderline symptoms as discussed in the section above on incest. The focus of the therapy remains on the rape and the client is referred for long-term treatment following CPT to begin dealing with her childhood issues. If the client is unable to focus on the rape issues, she is referred for long-term treatment to focus first on stabilization and coping skills. The rape can be processed later in therapy along with other traumatic events. If it is clear that the client cannot separate the rape from her other issues, we refer the client immediately to individual therapy, an incest group, or a program that specializes in the treatment of borderline personality (Linehan, in press).

We have not excluded women with avoidant or dependent personalities from either group or individual CPT. However, the therapist may find that women with either of these patterns present special management issues during treatment. The client with an avoidant personality tends to be very quiet in group format, denies or suppresses feelings, and is noncompliant with the homework assignments (or completes them superficially). The avoidance symptoms of PTSD tend to be compounded with a preexisting tendency to avoid distressing thoughts and feelings. Unless this type of client is challenged rather consistently, she will go through the motions of therapy without actually processing the rape cognitively or emotionally. Progress in therapy can be painfully slow.

The client with a dependent personality tends to rely too much on either the therapist or other group members in therapy. Because of their inability to trust their own judgment or feelings, these women attempt to elicit caretaking behavior from other people and express confusion about what they are feeling. It is not unusual for these women to telephone the therapist between sessions in order to be comforted, to elicit help in making decisions, or to validate accomplishments and feelings. In our experience, marital rape victims are the clients most likely to exhibit dependent personality disorder.

When working with a client with a dependent personality, it is important for the therapist to shape more self-reliant behavior by encouraging the client to identify and accept her own cognitions and feelings, as well as by reinforcing her efforts to make decisions and self-soothe. For example, one such client announced in group her belief that it is the therapist's job to be available whenever a client needs her. She demonstrated this expectation by calling the therapist on weekends between sessions. Another woman in the group challenged that assumption by stating that when she was unable to reach her individual therapist, she reminded herself that her therapist had a life of her own and would call back at the earliest convenient time. In the meantime, she tried to take care of herself by drawing on internal resources. As therapy progressed, the therapist increased the length of time before returning this client's phone calls. Before long, the client began to make her own decisions without waiting to talk to the therapist.

19

Therapist Considerations

❑ Therapist Gender

We are often asked if it is appropriate for male therapists to provide treatment for rape victims. Prior to developing CPT, we had male cotherapists provide other types of therapy in a group format (Resick, Jordan, Girelli, Hutter, & Marhoefer-Dvorak, 1988). Feedback from the clients was quite positive. Having a warm, empathic, male therapist helped the clients realize that some of their beliefs about men—for example, that all men were dangerous and that none could be trusted—were overgeneralized and inaccurate.

Male therapists also provide treatment to rape victims through our clinic. However, it is our policy to give the clients a choice of whether they wish to have a male or female therapist. Sometimes, the client is too phobic and uncomfortable to have a male therapist, and we respect her wishes. Male therapists often provide therapy to family members, husbands, and boyfriends of the rape victims.

Even when they are not providing direct therapy to the victim, a male therapist in the client's network may help change her overgeneralized beliefs about men.

❏ **Therapists' Attitudes and Beliefs**

Therapists can do a great deal of damage to clients if they hold negative beliefs about why women are raped or hold just-world beliefs. We have heard a multitude of stories about prior therapy our clients have received in which the therapist subtly blamed the victim or questioned, along with the client, whether the event was truly rape. These clients expressed great distress (once they found out that we did not blame them) at what they considered to be a betrayal on the part of their former therapist(s). One client expressed her reaction: "If this person is a trained therapist and she thought it was my fault, then it must have been." One therapist told her client that if she could not remember what happened, then it probably was not rape. The therapist obviously did not understand or was not aware of the dissociative reactions that occur frequently during and after events that are too horrifying to remember.

Prior to working with a rape victim, the therapist should examine his or her own beliefs. Until very recently, education about rape was unavailable and common myths prevailed in both the professional and lay literature. Common misperceptions about rape include (1) that women secretly or unconsciously wish to be overpowered; (2) that if a woman is raped, there must have been something wrong with her to begin with; (3) that a woman cannot be raped by someone she previously knew or had prior sexual relations with; and (4) that any healthy woman can stop rape from occurring. Furthermore, many people hold just-world beliefs that good things happen to good people and bad things happen to bad people. People, including therapists, may hold this belief even in the face of contradictory evidence in order to feel safe and immune from tragedy. Anytime a therapist asks "why" the client did or did not do something, there is an implication of victim blame. Rape victims are very sensitive to blame and are likely to interpret a why question as blaming even if the therapist's intentions are innocent.

It is easy for a therapist to view a client's behavior as foolhardy (hitchhiking, drinking with a new date) and become judgmental. However, it is important to remember that no matter what someone does or does not do, rape is not a justifiable consequence. Other people have behaved in the same way before and have not been raped. Careless behavior or provocative attire does not cause rape. The rapist has sole responsibility for his own behavior. If a therapist believes that victims cause rape, then he or she should not be working with victims in therapy; he or she will cause more harm than good.

❏ Secondary Traumatization

Hearing about the graphic details of rape or other acts of violence can be very distressing for therapists. Along with victims, you may have to accommodate your own schemata about the level of cruelty and violence of which humans are capable. Secondary trauma reactions, a parallel but less serious form of PTSD, are quite possible in therapists. McCann and Pearlman (1990b) have written about secondary traumatization and have differentiated it from countertransference or burnout. As a therapist, you may experience intrusive recollections or nightmares after hearing graphic accounts during the exposure component of CPT and may find yourself becoming more anxious or avoidant of situations you perceive as potentially dangerous (being home alone, driving at night, walking through parking garages, and so on). You may experience strong emotions such as sadness, anger, or disgust. It is also possible that you may experience disruptions in beliefs regarding yourself or others, particularly those that are already salient to you.

Therapist reactions may also be expressed in therapy with the victim. If therapists are uncomfortable hearing about the details of rape, they may subtly (or not so subtly) avoid going after these details in therapy. Rather than realizing that their own anxiety is interfering with therapy, therapists may rationalize their avoidance by saying they fear the client cannot handle this material or that it will be too overwhelming for her. It is important to remember that the client has been living with these details (albeit ineffectively) ever since the rape and that she needs to know that the memory is not too horrifying for the therapist(s) to accept.

These PTSD-like reactions are usually short-lived if therapists use the same therapeutic procedures with themselves as those they implement with the client. Therapists may need to find someone to talk to who can handle hearing about these events and the therapists' reactions. Peer or formal supervision is recommended when available. We also recommend reading the McCann and Pearlman article for additional thoughts on this topic.

20

Results of CPT

We have been collecting data on CPT participants for 4 years. At this point, we offer more group than individual treatment because, without outside funding, we have limited staffing. Chapter 16 discusses the potential advantages and disadvantages of each format for treatment. None of these treatment participants were recruited solely for the research. They were all treatment-seekers who were referred to us or were self-referred. At the time they called us seeking treatment, we determined whether they met the general criteria for participation. If so, they were informed of the study and invited to begin the assessment process. Final decisions about eligibility were made after the initial assessment session.

Criteria for participation include the following: (1) The women must have been raped at least 3 months prior to the first assessment; (2) if group participants, they cannot have a history of incest; and (3) they must have no severe competing pathology or active substance abuse. The participants were assessed four times: pretreatment, posttreatment, and 3 and 6 months posttreatment. The results from the first 19 group-format participants are presented in Resick and Schnicke (1992), where they are compared to another group of women who served as a waiting-list control group. The first four individually treated clients are presented in Resick (1992). Those subjects are included in the following analyses, as are 5 new individual treatment subjects and 17 women who have completed group therapy and the follow-up assessments since then.

At this time, 63 women have completed initial assessments. Of those, 7 were referred elsewhere because they were inappropriate and 5 were eligible but did not participate because they moved or had scheduling conflicts. Six women dropped out during treatment or before the first follow-up could be conducted (the dropout rate is 12%). In all, 45 women have completed CPT and at least two assessments, 36 in a group format and 9 in individual format. Thirty-one of the women completed 3- and 6-month follow-up assessments. All 9 individual treatment participants have completed all 4 assessments. Means and standard deviations for the group clients for each symptom scale at each session are presented in Table 20.1. Table 20.2 presents the means and standard deviations of the individually treated clients. Because of the differences in sample sizes, the two formats were not compared to each other.

❏ Group Treatment

The 36 women ranged in age from 19 to 45 ($M = 32.00$, $SD = 7.25$) and had some college on the average ($M = 14.58$ years of education, $SD = 2.25$). Thirty-three (91.67%) of the women were white, the other three African-American (8.33%). Thirty-three percent were married or cohabiting. The remainder were single (39%), divorced (17%), or separated (11%). Twenty-one women (58%) were raped once; nine (25%) were raped twice; one of the women was raped five times and the remaining four women (collapsed = 17%) were raped too many times to count in the context of ongoing relationships (see Figure 20.1). On the average, the women had experienced their most recent rape 8.21 years earlier ($SD = 8.58$ years; range = 3 months to 30 years).

Table 20.1 Means and standard deviations ( ) of CPT group-therapy
clients over time

Measure	Pre	Post	3 Months	6 Months
Impact of Event Scale				
Intrusion	18.69	9.83	11.23	10.65
	(9.28)	(7.99)	(10.67)	(8.19)
Avoidance	25.97	10.44	11.65	10.52
	(10.59)	(10.50)	(10.75)	(10.09)
PTSD Symptom Scale				
Reexperiencing	5.64	2.92	3.30	2.77
	(3.10)	(2.16)	(3.03)	(2.68)
Avoidance	12.47	5.56	6.50	5.77
	(5.48)	(4.47)	(5.04)	(4.58)
Arousal	11.08	5.28	5.50	5.48
	(4.76)	(4.01)	(4.98)	(4.89)
Beck Depression	22.75	11.06	9.48	9.87
Inventory	(10.05)	(8.18)	(7.57)	(8.71)
SCL-90-R				
Somatization	1.12	.66	.66	.61
	(.84)	(.47)	(11.74)	(.80)
Obsessive-Compulsive	1.79	1.04	1.03	.98
	(.99)	(.73)	(.85)	(.94)
Interpersonal Sensitivity	1.85	1.15	1.15	.98
	(.95)	(.86)	(.93)	(.86)
Depression	2.17	1.32	1.20	1.03
	(.90)	(.90)	(.83)	(.88)
Anxiety	1.73	.92	.91	.82
	(.94)	(.71)	(.77)	(.83)
Hostility	1.29	.85	.80	.87
	(.95)	(.83)	(.78)	(.82)
Phobic Anxiety	1.05	.52	.59	.58
	(.92)	(.69)	(.72)	(.87)
Paranoia	1.33	.91	.97	.82
	(.94)	(.76)	(.81)	(.83)
Psychoticism	1.07	.56	.55	.46
	(.70)	(.46)	(.52)	(.52)
PTSD	1.56	.89	.86	.78
	(.82)	(.63)	(.68)	(.74)
GSI	1.55	.92	.89	.81
	(.75)	(.57)	(.65)	(.70)
Hopelessness Scale				
Feel About Future	1.61	.50	.94	.87
	(1.91)	(1.23)	(1.50)	(1.34)
Loss of Motivation	2.14	.57	.61	.77
	(2.52)	(1.26)	(1.31)	(1.64)

Table 20.1 Continued

Measure	Pre	Post	3 Months	6 Months
Future Expectations	3.11	1.21	1.77	2.03
	(1.64)	(1.50)	(1.71)	(1.76)
Causal Dimension Scale				
Control by Others	9.61	12.72	12.10	14.23
	(5.65)	(5.76)	(5.23)	(3.89)
Control by You	6.86	3.72	3.29	3.80
	(4.35)	(3.47)	(2.58)	(2.73)
Internal-External	13.97	7.44	7.10	7.00
	(7.75)	(7.09)	(5.36)	(5.97)
Stable-Unstable	13.81	12.05	14.03	14.53
	(7.91)	(5.72)	(6.57)	(7.22)

Table 20.2 Means and standard deviations ( ) of CPT individual-therapy clients over time

Measure	Pre	Post	3 Months	6 Months
Impact of Event Scale				
Intrusion	22.67	4.00	9.44	9.33
	(6.24)	(3.94)	(6.89)	(9.14)
Avoidance	24.33	9.78	9.22	7.89
	(6.91)	(11.33)	(10.91)	(8.94)
PTSD Symptom Scale				
Reexperiencing	7.33	1.67	2.22	2.33
	(2.12)	(1.00)	(1.72)	(2.45)
Avoidance	12.00	3.00	3.11	4.11
	(4.97)	(2.45)	(2.42)	(3.10)
Arousal	12.11	4.33	4.22	6.11
	(3.48)	(3.00)	(3.23)	(4.23)
Beck Depression	21.44	6.22	6.78	9.22
Inventory	(8.02)	(5.63)	(6.34)	(8.93)
SCL-90-R				
Somatization	1.41	.56	.43	.64
	(.65)	(.38)	(.40)	(.46)
Obsessive-Compulsive	2.27	.63	.98	.91
	(.82)	(.39)	(.91)	(.83)
Interpersonal Sensitivity	1.60	.48	.39	.43
	(.78)	(.31)	(.47)	(.31)
Depression	2.15	.67	.56	.83
	(.85)	(.63)	(.47)	(.71)
Anxiety	1.98	.55	.67	.70
	(.67)	(.42)	(.55)	(.71)

Table 20.2 Continued

Measure	Pre	Post	3 Months	6 Months
Hostility	1.09	.43	.29	.52
	(.47)	(.46)	(.36)	(.60)
Phobic Anxiety	1.38	.27	.27	.38
	(.93)	(.26)	(.60)	(.61)
Paranoia	1.39	.44	.22	.46
	(.63)	(.22)	(.19)	(.30)
Psychoticism	1.03	.27	.09	.19
	(.52)	(.28)	(.14)	(.20)
PTSD	1.81	.51	.53	.62
	(.60)	(.38)	(.50)	(.48)
GSI	1.67	.50	.49	.61
	(.51)	(.33)	(.39)	(.40)
Hopelessness Scale				
Feel About Future	2.00	.33	.50	.44
	(2.12)	(.50)	(1.07)	(.73)
Loss of Motivation	2.00	.33	.25	.44
	(2.06)	(.71)	(.71)	(.88)
Future Expectations	3.67	1.67	1.75	1.56
	(1.58)	(1.32)	(1.39)	(1.42)
Causal Dimension Scale				
Control by Others	8.89	13.13	11.22	13.67
	(5.51)	(4.12)	(4.99)	(4.15)
Control by You	7.22	5.75	9.44	4.44
	(4.12)	(5.47)	(15.69)	(3.32)
Internal-External	16.78	9.13	8.89	9.11
	(9.74)	(7.90)	6.37	(7.08)
Stable-Unstable	14.00	9.63	11.22	10.11
	(6.48)	(6.50)	(6.91)	(4.73)

Results indicate that participants improved significantly from pre- to posttherapy on all symptom scales and most cognitive measures. Table 20.3 presents the results of MANOVAs and ANOVAs from pre- to posttherapy for the group therapy clients. There were marked improvements in scores on all measures except for one of the causal attribution scales: stable-unstable. Although they blamed themselves less and the assailant more, these women continued to believe that the rape was caused by stable conditions. Two other sets of analyses were conducted. First, scores from the 3-month follow-up were compared to scores from the posttherapy session.

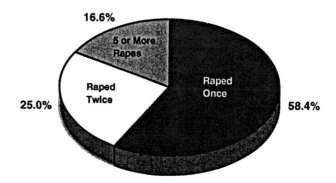

Figure 20.1. CPT Group Therapy Completers: Breakdown by Number of Rapes *N*=36

Table 20.3 Repeated Measures MANOVAs and ANOVAs on Outcome Measures for CPT Group-Therapy Recipients Pre- Versus Posttreatment

---

IES

	MANOVA:	$F(2,34) = 31.84, p < .0001$
		Wilks' Criterion = .35
	ANOVAs:	
Intrusion		$F(1,35) = 36.58, p < .0001$
Avoidance		$F(1,35) = 57.68, p < .0001$

PTSD-SS

	MANOVA:	$F(3,33) = 20.71, p < .0001$
		Wilks' Criterion = .35
ANOVAs:		
Reexperiencing		$F(1,35) = 39.36, p < .0001$
Avoidance		$F(1,35) = 45.99, p < .0001$
Arousal		$F(1,35) = 36.43, p < .0001$
BDI		$F(1,35) = 40.47, p < .0001$

SCL-90-R

	MANOVA:	$F(9,25) = 4.02, p < .0028$
		Wilks' Criterion = .32
	ANOVAs:	
Somatization		$F(1,35) = 14.95, p < .0005$
Obsessive-Compulsive		$F(1,35) = 23.47, p < .0001$
Interpersonal Sensitivity		$F(1,35) = 17.87, p < .0002$
Depression		$F(1,35) = 19.42, p < .0001$
Anxiety		$F(1,35) = 33.95, p < .0001$
Hostility		$F(1,35) = 5.00, p < .03$
Phobic Anxiety		$F(1,35) = 14.13, p < .0007$
Paranoid Ideation		$F(1,35) = 7.96, p < .008$
Psychoticism		$F(1,35) = 26.39, p < .0001$

Table 20.3 Continued

PTSD		$F(1,35) = 26.17, p <.0001$
GSI		$F(1,35) = 25.69, p <.0001$
Hopelessness Scale		
	MANOVA:	$F(3,25) = 12.00, p <.0001$
		Wilks' Criterion = .41
	ANOVAs:	
Feel About Future		$F(1,27) = 11.21, p <.0024$
Loss of Motivation		$F(1,27) = 12.21, p <.0017$
Future Expectations		$F(1,27) = 38.32, p <.0001$
Causal Dimension Scale		
	MANOVA:	$F(4,32) = 6.37, p <.0007$
		Wilks' Criterion = .54
	ANOVAs:	
Control by Others		$F(1,35) = 5.55, p <.0242$
Control by You		$F(1,35) = 13.98, p <.0007$
Internal-External		$F(1,35) = 16.09, p <.0003$
Stable-Unstable		$F(1,35) = 1.56, p <NS$

Next, scores from the 6-month session were compared to the post-therapy session. These analyses were nonsignificant, indicating that the subjects' improvements had been maintained over the 6-month follow-up period.

On the SCID interview (see Figure 20.2), 34 of the 36 women met full criteria for PTSD at the pretherapy assessment (the others were allowed to participate because they had severe levels of symptomatology and fully met 2 of the 3 criteria). Twenty-two of the women also met criteria for major depressive disorder. At the posttherapy assessment, only 4 women of the 36 still met criteria for PTSD and 5 met criteria for major depression. At the 3-month assessment, 4 of 30 women met criteria for PTSD and 2 met criteria for depression. At the 6-month follow-up, 2 of 29 women met criteria for PTSD and 3 met criteria for depression. Although 36 women completed treatment and the posttreatment assessment, we lost a few subjects between the post- and 6-month assessment sessions. Several of the clients moved after therapy and were unable to complete the SCID interview, although they did complete the self-report measures by mail. Five of the women dropped out completely between posttreatment and the 3-month follow-up.

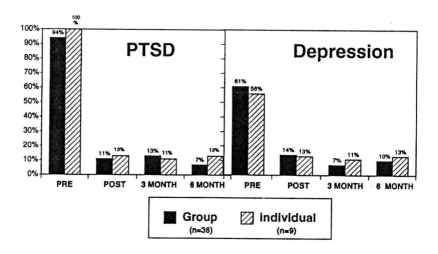

Figure 20.2. Effects of Cognitive Processing Therapy on Clinical Diagnoses

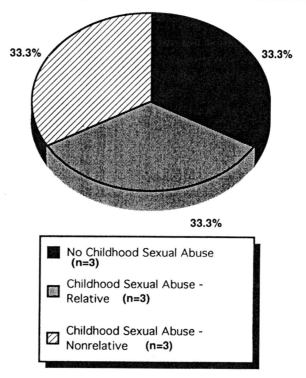

Figure 20.3. Individual CPT Completers: Breakdown by History of Childhood Sexual Abuse

❏ Individual Treatment

The demographics for the nine individual treatment subjects are as follows: mean age was 30.33 years (SD = 9.62); 78% were white; all were single, divorced, or separated; mean years of education was 13.44 (SD = 1.88); 55% had been raped once, and the other 44% had been raped twice. They had been raped an average of 4.8 years earlier (SD = 5.7 years; range = 5 months to 14.9 years). Six of the nine subjects had histories of childhood sexual abuse (see Figure 20.3).

The findings of the individual treatment subjects were very similar to the group-therapy subjects. Table 20.4 presents the results of the pretreatment and posttreatment analyses. The individual subjects scored significantly lower on all of the subscales at the posttherapy assessment except for a few of the cognitive scales on the Causal Dimension Scale. The individually treated clients became less internal in their causal beliefs about the rape, but they did not change with regard to controllability or stability of causes.

Most of the subscales were not significantly different between the posttherapy assessment and the 3- or 6-month follow-up. From posttreatment to the 3-month follow-up, there was a significant decrease in paranoia [$F(1,8)$ = 15.75, p <.005] and a trend on psychoticism scores [$F(1,8)$ = 5.22, p <.052], but an increase in intrusion [$F(1,8)$ = 12.54, p <.005] on the IES. The clients did not report increased intrusion on the PSS. The changes on these scales were not maintained at the 6-month follow-up. It is interesting to note that although they were experiencing more intrusive symptoms, the clients were probably labeling their experiences more accurately as fear reactions or flashbacks than as paranoia or psychotic reactions. There were no significant differences on any subscale between posttreatment scores and the 6-month follow-up.

On the SCID interview, all nine participants met full criteria for PTSD prior to treatment, and five met criteria for major depression (see Figure 20.2). At the posttreatment and follow-up assessments, only one of the individually treated subjects continued to report significant PTSD and depressive symptomatology. She was a recovering alcoholic who felt that if she stopped avoiding her memories and began experiencing her emotions, she would relapse into alcohol abuse. She completed only one third of the homework assignments.

Table 20.4 Repeated Measures MANOVAs and ANOVAs on Outcome Measures for CPT Individual Therapy Recipients Pre- Versus Posttreatment

IES

	MANOVA:	$F(2,7) = 39.01, p < .0002$
		Wilks' Criterion = .82
	ANOVAs:	
Intrusion		$F(1,8) = 88.34, p < .0001$
Avoidance		$F(1,8) = 13.47, p < .0063$

PTSD-SS

	MANOVA:	$F(3,6) = 27.18, p < .0007$
		Wilks' Criterion = .07
	ANOVAs:	
Reexperiencing		$F(1,8) = 96.33, p < .0001$
Avoidance		$F(1,8) = 20.39, p < .002$
Arousal		$F(1,8) = 28.00, p < .0007$
BDI		$F(1,8) = 22.99, p < .0014$

SCL-90-R

Somatization	$F(1,8) = 12.59, p < .0075$
Obsessive-Compulsive	$F(1,8) = 38.88, p < .0002$
Interpersonal Sensitivity	$F(1,8) = 14.98, p < .0047$
Depression	$F(1,8) = 20.60, p < .0019$
Anxiety	$F(1,8) = 36.09, p < .0003$
Hostility	$F(1,8) = 9.49, p < .0151$
Phobic Anxiety	$F(1,8) = 15.33, p < .0044$
Paranoid Ideation	$F(1,8) = 21.47, p < .0017$
Psychoticism	$F(1,8) = 17.06, p < .0033$
PTSD	$F(1,8) = 39.16, p < .0002$
GSI	$F(1,8) = 34.93, p < .0004$

Hopelessness Scale

	MANOVA:	$F(3,6) = 5.63, p < .0352$
		Wilks' Criterion = .26
	ANOVAs:	
Feel About Future		$F(1,8) = 7.14, p < .0282$
Loss of Motivation		$F(1,8) = 10.00, p < .0133$
Future Expectations		$F(1,8) = 16.00, p < .0039$

Causal Dimension Scale

	ANOVAs:	
Control by Others		$F(1,8) = 1.72, p < NS$
Control by You		$F(1,8) = 2.57, p < NS$
Internal-External		$F(1,8) = 5.92, p < .0452$
Stable-Unstable		$F(1,8) = 3.14, p < NS$

❑ Conclusions

Overall, CPT is performing very well. Using the SCID interview, 96% of the women met criteria for PTSD at pretreatment. At post-treatment, 88.4% of the women did not meet the full criteria for PTSD (38 of 43 who met full criteria initially). Of the 38 women who have received the SCID at the 6-month follow-up (several were unavailable for interviewing), only 3 (8%) still met full criteria for PTSD. At pretreatment, 60% of the women (27 of 45) met full criteria for depression, while at follow-up assessments 14% were depressed 1 week following treatment (6 of 44 women interviewed), 7.7% were depressed at 3 months after therapy (3 of 39 interviewed), and 11% were depressed at the 6-month assessment session (4 of 37 women interviewed).

On the cognitive measure, the Hopelessness Scale, the results indicated lasting changes in cognitions following treatment. Sub-jects improved significantly on all three factors (feelings about the future, loss of motivation, and future expectations), from pre- to posttherapy. There were no significant changes from posttreatment to 3 or 6 months follow-up. The women are reporting more optimis-tic beliefs about their futures. They also reported lasting changes in their causal attributions about the crime. Specifically, after treatment they attributed more causal control to others and less to themselves and greater external attributions for the crime.

The results we have obtained thus far are quite encouraging. The vast majority of clients improved markedly after completing CPT. These findings are particularly encouraging considering that these clients have been suffering from chronic PTSD and depression, and some have been raped multiple times. While the early sessions of treatment are emotion-filled and intense, our dropout rate during treatment is quite low. The therapy, as it currently exists, is only 12 sessions long, so the treatment is efficient as well as effective.

References

American Psychiatric Association. (1980). *Diagnostic and statistical manual of mental disorders* (3rd ed.). Washington, DC: Author.

American Psychiatric Association (1987). *Diagnostic and statistical manual of mental disorders* (3rd ed., revised). Washington, DC: Author.

Atkeson, B., Calhoun, K. S., Resick, P. A., & Ellis, E. (1982). Victims of rape: Repeated assessment of depressive symptoms. *Journal of Consulting and Clinical Psychology, 50*, 96-102.

Beck, A. T., & Emery, G. (1985). *Anxiety disorders and phobias: A cognitive perspective.* New York: Basic Books.

Beck, A. T., Rush, A. J., Shaw, B. F., & Emery, G. (1979). *Cognitive therapy of depression.* New York: Guilford.

Beck, A. T., Ward, C. H., Mendelson, M., Mock, J., & Erbaugh, J. (1961). An inventory for measuring depression. *Archives of General Psychiatry, 4*, 561-571.

Beck, A. T., Weissman, A., Lester, D., & Trexler, L. (1974). The measurement of pessimism: The Hopelessness Scale. *Journal of Consulting and Clinical Psychology, 42*, 861-865.

Becker, J. V., Abel, G. G., & Skinner, L. J. (1979). The impact of a sexual assault on the victim's sexual life. *Victimology: An International Journal, 4*, 229-235.

Calhoun, K. S., Atkeson, B. N., & Resick, P. A. (1982). A longitudinal examination of fear reactions in victims of rape. *Journal of Counseling Psychology, 29*, 655-661.

Chemtob, C., Roitblat, H. L., Hamada, R. S., Carlson, J. G., & Twentyman, C. T. (1988). A cognitive action theory of post-traumatic stress disorder. *Journal of Anxiety Disorders, 2*, 253-275.

Derogatis, L. R. (1977). *SCL-90: Administration, scoring and procedure manual-I for the R (revised) version.* Baltimore: Johns Hopkins University School of Medicine.

Ellis, A., & Harper, R. A. (1975). *A new guide to rational living.* North Hollywood, CA: Wilshire.

Ellis, E. M., Atkeson, B. M., & Calhoun, K. S. (1981). An assessment of long-term reaction to rape. *Journal of Abnormal Psychology, 90*, 263-266.

Foa, E. B., & Kozak, M. J. (1986). Emotional processing of fear: Exposure to corrective information. *Psychological Bulletin, 99*, 20-35.

Foa, E. B., Riggs, D. S., Dancu, C. V., & Rothbaum, B. O. (in press). Reliability and validity of a brief instrument for assessing post-traumatic stress disorder. *Journal of Traumatic Stress.*

Foa, E. B., Rothbaum, B. O., Riggs, D. S., & Murdock, T. B. (1991). Treatment of Post-Traumatic Stress Disorder in rape victims: A comparison between cognitive-behavioral procedures and counseling. *Journal of Consulting and Clinical Psychology, 59* (5), 715-723.

Foa, E. B., Steketee, G., & Rothbaum, B. O. (1989). Behavioral/cognitive conceptualizations of post-traumatic stress disorder. *Behavior Therapy, 20*, 155-176.

Frank, E., Anderson, B., Stewart, B. D., Dancu, C., Hughes, C., & West, D. (1988). Efficacy of cognitive behavior therapy and systematic desensitization in the treatment of rape trauma. *Behavior Therapy, 19*, 403-420.

Frank, E., & Stewart, B. D. (1984). Depressive symptoms in rape victims: A revisit. *Journal of Affective Disorders, 7*, 77-85.

Frank, E., Turner, S. M., & Duffy, B. (1979). Depressive symptoms in rape victims. *Journal of Affective Disorders, 1*, 269-277.

Hollon, S. D., & Garber, J. (1988). Cognitive therapy. In L. Y. Abramson (Ed.), *Social cognition and clinical psychology: A synthesis* (pp. 204-253). New York: Guilford.

Horowitz, M. J. (1976). *Stress response syndromes.* New York: Jason Aronson.

Horowitz, M. J., Wilner, N., & Alvarez, W. (1979). Impact of event scale: A measure of subjective stress. *Psychosomatic Medicine, 41*, 209-218.

Jones, J. C., & Barlow, D. H. (1990). The etiology of posttraumatic stress disorder. *Clinical Psychology Review, 10*, 299-328.

Kilpatrick, D. G., Best, C. L., Veronen, J. L., Amick, A. E., Villeponteaux, L. A., & Ruff, G. A. (1985). Mental health correlates of criminal victimization: A random community survey. *Journal of Consulting and Clinical Psychology, 53*, 866-873.

Kilpatrick, D. G., & Calhoun, K. S. (1988). Early behavioral treatment for rape trauma: Efficacy or artifact? *Behavior Therapy, 19*, 421-427.

Kilpatrick, D. G., Resick, P. A., & Veronen, L. J. (1981). Effects of a rape experience: A longitudinal study. *Journal of Social Issues, 37*, 105-121.

Kilpatrick, D. G., Saunders, B. E., Veronen, L. J., Best, C. L., & Von, J. M. (1987). Criminal victimization: Lifetime prevalence, reporting to police, and psychological impact. *Crime and Delinquency, 33*, 479-489.

Kilpatrick, D. G., & Veronen, L. J. (1984, February). *Treatment of fear and anxiety in victims of rape.* Final report of NIMH, Grant No. MH29602.

Kilpatrick, D. G., Veronen, L. J., Saunders, B. E., Best, C. L., Amick-McMullan, A. E., & Paduhovich, J. L. (1987). *The psychological impact of crime: A study of randomly studied crime victims*. Final report of NIJ Grant No. 84-IJ-CX-0039. Washington, DC: National Institute of Justice.

Koss, M. P. (1985). The hidden rape victim: Personality, attitudinal, and situational characteristics. *Psychology of Women Quarterly, 9*, 193-212.

Koss, M. P., Gidycz, C. A., & Wisniewski, N. (1987). The scope of rape: Incidence and prevalence of sexual aggression and victimization in a national sample of higher education students. *Journal of Consulting and Clinical Psychology, 55*, 162-170.

Lang, P. J. (1977). Imagery in therapy: An information processing analysis of fear. *Behavior Therapy, 8*, 862-886.

Lerner, M. J., & Miller, D. T. (1978). Just world research and the attribution process: Looking back and ahead. *Psychological Bulletin, 85*, 1030-1051.

Linehan, M. M. (in press). *Cognitive behavior therapy of borderline personality disorder.* New York: Guilford.

McCann, I. L., & Pearlman, L. A. (1990a). *Psychological trauma and the adult survivor: Theory, therapy, and transformation.* New York: Brunner/Mazel.

McCann, I. L., & Pearlman, L. A. (1990b). Vicarious traumatization: A framework for understanding the psychological effects of working with victims. *Journal of Traumatic Stress, 3*, 131-149.

McCann, I. L., Sakheim, D. K., & Abrahamson, D. J. (1988). Trauma and victimization: A model of psychological adaptation. *The Counseling Psychologist, 16*, 531-594.

Murphy, S. M., Amick-McMullan, A. E., Kilpatrick, D. G., Haskett, M. E., Veronen, L. J., Best, C. L., & Saunders, B. E. (1988). Rape victims' self-esteem: A longitudinal analysis. *Journal of Interpersonal Violence, 3*, 355-370.

Resick, P. A. (1988). *Reactions of female and male victims of rape or robbery.* Final report of Grant No. 85-IJ-CX-0042. Washington, DC: National Institute of Justice.

Resick, P. A. (1990). Victims of sexual assault. In A. J. Lurigio, W. G. Skogan, & R. C. Davis (Eds.), *Victims of crime: Problems, policies, and programs* (pp. 69-86). (Vol. 25 of Sage Criminal Justice System Annuals.) Newbury Park, CA: Sage.

Resick, P. A. (1992). Cognitive treatment of crime-related post-traumatic stress disorder. In R. Peters & R. McMahon (Eds.), *Aggression and violence throughout the life span* (171-191). Newbury Park, CA: Sage.

Resick, P. A., Jordan, C. G., Girelli, S. A., Hutter, C. H., & Marhoefer-Dvorak, S. (1988). A comparative outcome study of behavioral group therapy for sexual assault victims. *Behavior Therapy, 19*, 385-401.

Resick, P. A., & Schnicke, M. K. (1990). Treating symptoms in adult victims of sexual assault. *Journal of Interpersonal Violence, 5* (4), 488-506.

Resick, P. A., & Schnicke, M. K. (1992). Cognitive processing therapy for sexual assault victims. *Journal of Consulting and Clinical Psychology, 60*, 748-756.

Resnick, H. S., Kilpatrick, D. G., Saunders, B. E., & Best, C. L. (1991, November). *Crime-related post-traumatic stress disorder in a representative national sample of women: Prevalence and etiological factors.* Paper presented at 25th annual meeting of the Association for the Advancement of Behavior Therapy, New York.

Rothbaum, B. O., Foa, E. B., Riggs, D. S., Murdock, T., & Walsh, W. (1992). A prospective examination of posttraumatic stress disorder in rape victims. *Journal of Traumatic Stress, 5*(3), 455-475.

Russell, D. (1982). The causal dimension scale: A measure of how individuals perceive causes. *Journal of Personality and Social Psychology, 42*, 1137-1145.

Russell, D. E. H. (1984). *Sexual exploitation: Rape, child sexual abuse, and workplace harassment.* Beverly Hills, CA: Sage.

Saunders, B. E., Arata, C. M., & Kilpatrick, D. G. (1990). Development of a crime-related post-traumatic stress disorder scale for women within the Symptom Checklist-90-Revised. *Journal of Traumatic Stress, 3,* 439-448.

Shields, N. M., Resick, P. A., & Hanneke, C. R. (1990). Victims of marital rape. In R. T. Ammerman & M. Hersen (Eds.), *Treatment of family violence: A sourcebook* (pp. 165-182). New York: John Wiley.

Spitzer, R. L., Williams, J. B. W., & Gibbons, M. (1987). *Structured clinical interview for DSM-III-Non-patient Version (SCID-NP-V).* New York: Biometrics Research Department, New York State Psychiatric Institute.

Williams, J. M. G., Watts, F. N., MacLeod, C., & Mathews, A. (1988). *Cognitive psychology and emotional disorders.* New York: John Wiley.

Wolpe, J. (1969). *The practice of behavior therapy.* Elmsford, NY: Pergamon.

About the Authors

Patricia A. Resick, Ph.D., received her doctorate in clinical psychology from the University of Georgia in 1976. She is currently Professor of Psychology and Director of the Center for Trauma Recovery at the University of Missouri-St. Louis. Her research has focused on assessment and treatment of victims of crime, with emphasis on post-traumatic stress disorder and depression in rape victims. She has received several grants from the National Institute of Mental Health and the National Institute of Justice.

Monica K. Schnicke, M.A., is a graduate student at the University of Missouri-St. Louis in the clinical psychology doctoral program. She is currently an intern at the St. Louis Veterans Administration Medical Center and is working on completing research requirements for her degree. Her research interests include post-traumatic stress disorder, adult survivors of sexual abuse, and attributions following traumatic events. While working with Professor Resick, she conducted both individual and group therapy with rape victims using cognitive processing therapy.

Linda M. Housman, M.A., is a graduate student at the University of Missouri-St. Louis in the clinical psychology doctoral program. Her research interests are in the general area of victimization, including sexual assault and therapist sexual misconduct. As an assistant to Professor Resick on the Crime Victim Recovery Project, she has been cotherapist for several rape trauma therapy groups.

CPSIA information can be obtained
at www.ICGtesting.com
Printed in the USA
FFOW04n2221040115
10013FF